EXERCISE BOOKLET

THE COLLEGE WRITER'S HANDBOOK

Vici Casana

EXERCISE BOOKLET

THE COLLEGE WRITER'S HANDBOOK
First Edition

THE COLLEGE WRITER
Second Edition

Randall VanderMey
Westmont College

Verne Meyer
Dordt College

John Van Rys
Redeemer University College

Pat Sebranek

HOUGHTON MIFFLIN COMPANY   BOSTON   NEW YORK

Publisher: Patricia A. Coryell
Editor in Chief: Suzanne Phelps Weir
Senior Development Editor: Judith Fifer
Assistant Editor: Anne Leung
Project Editor: Robin Hogan
Senior Manufacturing Buyer: Karen Fawcett
Senior Marketing Manager: Cindy Graff Cohen

Printed in the U.S.A.

ISBN-10: 0-618-49171-6
ISBN-13: 978-0-618-49171-1

123456789-VHO-10 09 08 07 06

CONTENTS

	Part 8	Multilingual and ESL Guidelines 147

PREFACE

The exercises in this booklet are designed to accompany *The College Writer's Handbook* and *The College Writer,* second edition. The numbers of the exercise sets correspond to the chapters in *The College Writer's Handbook*, but please refer to the table of contents on pages v–viii for the specific corresponding section. Also, the table of contents provides the corresponding chapter in *The College Writer,* second edition.

Instructors who have adopted either *The College Writer's Handbook* or *The College Writer,* second edition, are welcome to photocopy these exercises as needed. The *Exercise Booklet* is also available for student purchase.

To make it easy for students to check their own work, we have provided the Answer Key to Lettered Exercises at the end of this booklet. The Answer Key to Numbered Exercises are password-protected on the instructor Websites for both textbooks **www.thecollegewriter.com** and from there, instructors can choose to print out the answers for grading or to distribute copies to students.

Students can write their answers and make their revisions directly on the pages of this booklet. The perforated pages may then be torn out and submitted to the instructor. Students can also work independently, in class or at home, self-checking their work by consulting the answer keys.

THE COLLEGE WRITER'S HANDBOOK

PART 3
STYLE ISSUES

12.1   IDENTIFYING TOPIC, RESTRICTING, AND SUPPORTING SENTENCES

Directions: In the following four paragraphs, identify each type of sentence on the write-on line that precedes it. Use **T** for the topic sentence, **S** for a sentence that provides supporting detail, and **R** for a sentence that restricts the paragraph's topic.*

Example:

___*T*___ The soft-drink business is in transition.   ___*R*___ Recent introductions of noncaffeine colas and of new artificial sweeteners for diet drinks have created new markets.   ___*S*___ Research indicates that these new markets are likely to grow well into the next decade.   ___*S*___ Soft-drink producers who ignore these trends will soon face lower profits.

* The division of paragraphs into topic, restriction, and illustration slots from A. L. Becker, "A Tagmemic Approach to Paragraph Analysis," reprinted in *The Sentence and the Paragraph* (Urbana, IL: NCTE, 1966), 33–38.

A.   _____ The best-known sultan is probably Suleyman the Magnificent, who expanded the [Ottoman] bounds and came close to capturing Vienna in the sixteenth century. _____ History shows contrary sides of Suleyman. _____ A Venetian envoy described him as "by nature melancholy, much addicted to women, liberal, proud, hasty, and yet sometimes very gentle." _____ He wrote poetry under the pen name *Muhibbi* and remained devoted for many years to a Ukrainian concubine named Roxelana, whom he married. _____ In one poem, he describes Roxelana, who took the name *Hurrem* after her conversion to Islam, as "My sheer delight, my revelry, my feast, my torch, my sunshine, my sun in heaven; / My orange, my pomegranate, the flaming candle that lights up my pavilion." _____ Often called the Lawgiver, Suleyman codified and simplified a complex and confusing array of legal procedures. _____ His code attempted to wipe out discriminatory practices against Christian subjects and eased the draconian punishments against criminals.

Stanley Meisler, " Splendors of Topkapi,"
Smithsonian, February 2000: 121.

B.   _____ Professional boxing is too brutal a sport for any civilized people to tolerate. _____ In the ring, boxers routinely treat spectators to the sight of bruised skin, bloodied noses, torn lips, and swollen eyes. _____ Mike Tyson bit off part of his opponent's ear. _____ Ray "Boom Boom" Mancini even treated viewers to the death of his opponent. _____ But the damage boxers inflict upon each other is not limited to injuries evident in the ring. _____ Sugar Ray Leonard had his career shortened by a torn retina in the right eye. _____ Muhammad Ali is now suffering from a form of Parkinson's disease caused, many doctors believe, by too many blows to the head.

1.   _____ The other emotional ingredients of conscience are that quaint pair, guilt and shame. _____ Although some child advocates insist that no child should ever be shamed, scientists who study moral development disagree. _____ "Guilt and shame are part of conscience," says Berkowitz. _____ In young children, the sense of right and wrong is born of the feeling that you have disappointed someone you love, usually your parents. _____ If there is no one whose love you need, whose disapproval breaks your heart, you are missing a crucial source of the emotions that add up to knowing right from wrong and acting on it.

Sharon Begley and Claudia Kalb, "Learning Right
from Wrong," *Newsweek,* 13 March 2000: 31.

2.   _____ It's not just in behavioral laboratories that animals display their cognitive powers, but also in the wild. _____ In fact, field biologists are finding that many species' natural behaviors are no less complex than the ones that psychologists are going to such lengths to teach them. _____ Research has shown, for example, that the calls of some free-ranging monkeys are not just raw expressions of arousal, as was long assumed, but fairly detailed reports about events in the outside world. _____

Robert Syfarth and Dorothy Cheney of the University of Pennsylvania have found that vervet monkeys in Kenya have at least three distinct alarm calls—one for snakes, one for eagles, one for leopards—and that each one elicits a different response.

Geoffrey Cowley, "The Wisdom of Animals," *Newsweek*, 28 May 1988: 56–57.

12.2 STAYING ON THE TOPIC

Directions: In the blank at the bottom of each paragraph, write the number of any sentence that is digressive. Any paragraph may contain up to three digressive sentences.

Example:

(1) To use a library efficiently, one must first learn how books are classified in the computerized catalog. (2) These catalogs are usually located on a library's main floor—but they are not always. (3) Books are listed in three ways: by author, by title, and by subject. (4) Therefore, if one knows a title, but not an author or a subject, one can still easily locate a book.

_____*2*_____

A.   (1) To see the Grand Canyon as it should be seen, a visitor must rise before dawn. (2) The canyon is located in northern Arizona. (3) Just before the sun appears, the walls of the canyon are a deep purple, and a visitor almost feels the eerie silence. (4) Gradually the canyon comes alive. (5) Soon there are the cries of a few birds. (6) Then with the first streaks of light, the rocks begin to glow in rich oranges and reds. (7) Finally, the details appear—the deep crevices, the patches of grass and mesquite and sage—and a visitor who looks closely may see a deer or chipmunk. (8) Later the visitor can visit the many shops located near Bright Angel Lodge and El Tovar.

_____

B.   (1) Every ten years, the Census Bureau undertakes the Herculean task of counting the estimated 275 million residents of the United States. (2) It begins by mailing questionnaires to every household. (3) It also blankets the nation with advertisements that explain how the census benefits communities. (4) For many reasons, however, a large percentage of the population never returns these forms. (5) Other countries are more successful in gathering similar data. (6) The bureau then sends out thousands of temporary workers who make personal calls and even interview neighbors in an effort to document as many residents as possible. (7) Despite these efforts, a large number of residents are never counted.

_____

C. (1) Marathon swimmers are a distinct breed. (2) Unlike most athletes, they are stocky rather than lithe. (3) Relatively large amounts of body fat help them float as well as insulate them from frigid water. (4) As their muscular physiques attest, Olympic-style swimmers train for bursts of speed. (5) Covering distances of one to sixty miles, marathon swimmers must be able to tolerate unusual amounts of physical pain and psychological stress. (6) In addition to nausea, jellyfish stings, and hypothermia, they must be able to endure prolonged exposure to salt water that can transform their faces into grotesque masks. (7) They must be able to shake off hallucinations that tease or terrify them as they approach the limits of human endurance. (8) Needless to say, sheer doggedness is their strongest instinct.

_____

D. (1) Archaeology is a much more exact science than many people realize. (2) For example, archaeologists have determined that on a day in late spring approximately 400,000 years ago, about twenty-five people made a visit to a cove on the Mediterranean coast near Nice, France. (3) From the study of fossil bones, stone tools, various imprints in the sand, and the density of the sand, scientists have reconstructed in detail much of the three-day sojourn. (4) Imprints give clues to where these ancient people slept and what they slept on. (5) Archaeology has really matured as a science and has become quite popular in the public's eye since Heinrich Schliemann's excavation of ancient cities in the late nineteenth century. (6) These imaginative scientists also know much about the food these nomadic people ate, how they prepared it, how they hunted for food, and how they protected the group from predators at night. (7) The human imagination simply has no limits.

_____

E.   (1) The modern photographer needs more than a simple developing kit to process photographs at home. (2) Actually, developing them at home is probably more expensive than sending them to professional laboratories to develop them. (3) The most important and most expensive item required for film processing is a good enlarger. (4) If one develops negatives without an enlarger, the final pictures are almost too small to enjoy. (5) Used enlargers for sale are very difficult to find. (6) Furthermore, one should purchase an enlarging easel, an enlarger timer, and a focusing lens. (7) Only after buying this relatively expensive equipment can the amateur photographer hope to develop good-quality prints.

_____

1.   (1) Financial aid for students includes basic grants, work-study jobs, scholarships, and loans. (2) In the past, students who required financial assistance often had to drop out of school and work for a few months. (3) Many students simultaneously receive aid from several of these sources, usually combining scholarships with work-study programs. (4) College administrators continually solicit alumni for more money. (5) Jobs are especially popular because they may provide valuable experience for a future vocation. (6) Some of the country's most distinguished citizens received scholarships. (7) All students in need of financial assistance qualify for aid in one form or another. (8) Even if they must borrow from university loan funds, they usually pay only minimal interest charges. (9) Students who desire assistance should contact their school's financial aid office for additional information.

_____

2.   (1) Not all cookies are good to eat. (2) Electronic "cookies"—identification numbers silently implanted in your computer when you visit certain Web sites—threaten to make privacy a thing of the past. (3) Admittedly, cookies do have some benefits. (4) They remember your password when you return to a favorite site, and they are the technology that allows you to build a "shopping cart" when you buy items online. (5) As computer sales increase, so will the number of cookies. (6)

Without careful restriction, though, cookies will let electronic businesses know, record, and even sell lists of every Web site you have ever visited. (7) Worse yet, a record of your Internet habits could be used in the future by insurance companies, lawyers, or even personal enemies.

———————

3.   (1) Sunscreen and suntan lotion are modern inventions that were originally designed for GIs stationed in the Pacific during World War II. (2) The enemy in the Pacific theater was Japan. (3) These lotions popularized the modern phenomenon of sunbathing, which, although considered fashionable by some, is in reality dangerous. (4) Until the 1920s, most Americans lived inland and rarely visited the beach. (5) With the ozone layer being depleted, the use of sunscreen lotion is vital. (6) Researchers have found that overexposure to the sun causes skin cancer in later life; therefore, a sunburn is more than a painful inconvenience—it is a health hazard.

———————

4.   (1) Each year thousands of Americans fly across the country with their pets. (2) With a little forethought, these owners can reduce the stress their favorite animal will experience in flight. (3) The best way to transport smaller pets is in a cage designed to fit beneath a plane seat. (4) Fellow travelers may be allergic to animal hair and dander. (5) Larger pets will have to travel in the cargo section. (6) An article of clothing permeated with the owner's scent can help calm them in this unfamiliar setting.

———————

5.   (1) *El Niño*, the name given to warm currents that flow past the coasts of eastern South America, is a mixed blessing in the Western Hemisphere. (2) On the one hand, these currents bring rain to the arid coasts of Peru and Ecuador, and this usually barren region bursts into life with the arrival of badly needed moisture. (3) Further north, though, the same weather phenomenon brings floods that

destroy crops, roads, bridges, and neighborhoods. (4) In addition, the southeastern United States is abnormally dry during these years. (5) These currents also coincide with droughts in parts of Australia and Southeast Asia.

12.3 ARRANGING YOUR DETAILS (ORGANIZATIONAL STRATEGIES)

Directions: Identify the type of organizational pattern (analogy, cause and effect, chronological order, classification, comparison and contrast, climax, definition, illustration, narration, or process) used in each of the following paragraphs on the line below the paragraph.

Example:

With a diminished ozone layer, more UV [ultraviolet radiation] from the sun will reach the earth. Scientists believe that more UV will induce mutations in the organisms that anchor the food chain of the world's oceans. UV threatens not only to cause more cases of skin cancer but also to damage the immune system, a blow that could leave us defenseless against infectious diseases. More UV may damage crops worth billions of dollars. "It is no exaggeration to say that the health and safety of millions of people around the world are at stake," says David Doniger of the Natural Resources Defense Council.

Sharon Begley, "A Gaping Hole in the Sky," *Newsweek*, 11 July 1988: 21.

cause and effect

A. Amid five acres of paddocks, pens, and fields stands a sturdy roundhouse, more than forty feet in diameter and thirty feet high, its basketwork walls plastered with daub. The thatched, conical roof, where swallows nest, protects ovens and querns and crockery. Immediately outside are several haystacks and a byre. A low bank and a shallow dyke enclose the central compound. Beyond lie fields of wheat, barley, beans, and flax. In outlying pastures livestock graze—unusual breeds of sheep and cattle, gamey and hirsute.

Cullen Murphy, "The Buster Experiment," *The Atlantic*, August 1985: 20.

B. The male eagle is a model husband for these times. He does his share of home building by gathering sticks—often six feet long—for the base of the nest. Barreling into the desired branch at full speed, he hits it with his feet, grabs it with his talons as it cracks, and flies away with it. He takes his turn sitting on the nest and helps feed and care for the newborns. According to Hodges's current study, one of the parents remains at the nest constantly until the eaglets are four weeks old.

> Sharon Begley, "Comeback for a National Symbol," *Newsweek*, 9 July 1984: 65.

C. As strange as it may seem, modern biochemistry has shown that the cell is operated by machines—literally, molecular machines. Like their man-made counterparts (such as mousetraps, bicycles, and space shuttles), molecular machines range from the simple to the enormously complex: mechanical, force-generating machines, like those in muscles; electronic machines, like those in nerves; and solar-powered machines, like those of photosynthesis. Of course, molecular machines are made primarily of proteins, not metal and plastic. In this chapter, I will discuss molecular machines that allow cells to swim, and you will see what is required for them to do so.

> Michael J. Behe, *Darwin's Black Box* (New York: Touchstone, 1996), 51.

D. One good way to knead is to push hard into the dough with both heels of your hands and then pull the top edge toward you so that it looks like the crest of a wave. When the dough is too stiff to be stirred, it's ready to be kneaded. Cover a flat surface and your hands with flour, keeping track of how much you use by taking it from the remaining cup or so. Knead more flour in by tablespoons, adding it as the white powder disappears.

> Corby Kummer, "Parlor Pizza," *The Atlantic*, April 1985: 129.

E.   College will always convey a certain image: Gothic buildings filled with postadolescents listening to tweed-clad professors. But the Internet is blurring the picture, and State U is quietly morphing into College.com. To be sure, a virtual university is no place for Felicity or her just-out-of-high-school friends; they want the full college package, kegs and all. But "typical" college students—18–22 years old, living in dorms, studying full time—make up only 16 percent of enrollment today, says Arthur Levine, president of Teachers College at Columbia University. They're far outnumbered by the 79 percent of adults who lack diplomas. Many of these folks have kids, work irregular hours or travel, which makes night school impossible. The result: millions of adults are dialing for diplomas. They're attending start-up schools you've never heard of—and prestigious ones like Columbia, Stanford, and Duke. By the end of the year, according to researchers at InterEd, 75 percent of all U.S. universities will offer online course work, and 5.8 million students will have logged on. Study anytime! College has never been so convenient.

Daniel McGinn, "College Online," *Newsweek*,
24 April 2000: 56.

1.   To my biased taste, Cantonese cuisine is the greatest of all Chinese cookery. The classical Cantonese style emphasizes freshness of ingredients and subtle but distinct contrasts of tastes and textures. A single dish is often composed of sweet and sour flavors, crisp and creamy or crunchy and tender textures, and hot and cold temperatures. Gentle, quick cooking preserves the delicate neutral flavors, colors, and aromas of this fresh food. Soy, hoisin, and oyster sauces—all relatively mild and congenial—are its mainstays. There is not an overdose of garlic, sharp spices, and heavy oils. It is definitely not greasy.

Ken Hom, "The Road to Canton," *The New York Times Magazine*, 5 June 1988: 57.

2. In American English there are three main regional types—Northern, Midland, and Southern—with a good many different blendings of these as one travels westward. . . . There are also a number of subtypes on the Atlantic Coast, such as the speech of the New York and Boston areas in the North and the Charleston-Savannah area in the South. All types of American English have grown out of the regional modifications of the British Standard—with some coloring from the British dialects—as it existed in the seventeenth century, when it was much less rigid than it is today.

    Thomas Pyles, *The Origins and Development of the English Language*, 2nd ed. (New York: Harcourt, 1971), 235.

3. For a maximum fruit production, use a wire trellis; it provides the best support for muscadines. To build a trellis, first drive a 4- to 5-foot stake into the ground beside the vine at planting time. Then, when the vine starts growing, select the strongest shoot to become the main stem and tie it to the stake. During the first summer, remove all side shoots. When the stem reaches the top of the stake, pinch off its tip to encourage growth of the side shoots.

    Steve Bender, "The Not-So-Lowly Muscadine," *Progressive Farmer,* July 1988: 59.

4. I see several advantages to reintegrating grammar into the writing curriculum under this new conception of its role. First, teachers have an incentive to teach it more frequently and with more enthusiasm. Second, the public can take heart that we are getting "back to basics" at last. As always, of course, some people will not learn even the handbook rules; some will learn those and nothing more; and some will find the handbook rules a help in learning the real grammar of the English

language. Perhaps more students will learn to write grammatical prose, but that is less important than that more students may discover what it means to write well.

Geoffrey Nunberg, "An Apology for Grammar,"
National Forum, Fall 1985: 15.

5.   Even the kindest and most well-intentioned parent will sometimes become exasperated. The difference between the good and the not-so-good parent in such situations is that the good parent will realize that his exasperation probably has more to do with himself than with what the child did, and that showing his exasperation will not be to anyone's advantage. The not-so-good parent, in contrast, believes that his exasperation was caused only by his child and that therefore he has every right to act on it.

Bruno Bettelheim, "Punishment Versus Discipline,"
The Atlantic, November 1985: 52.

12.4   USING TRANSITIONS AND REPETITION

Directions: In each of the following paragraphs, underline all transition words, linking words, and instances of repetition.

Example:

All <u>moose</u> are of a single circumpolar species, *Alces alces,* found in most of Canada, northern Russia, a corner of Poland, <u>and</u> parts of Scandinavia, <u>as well as</u> Alaska <u>and</u> the previously mentioned states. <u>In Sweden</u>, <u>moose</u> are so plentiful in some areas that <u>they</u> pose a serious traffic hazard. The same is true in parts of Alaska. <u>On the Kenai peninsula</u>, as many as 250 <u>moose</u> have been killed on the highways in one year. <u>But</u> <u>although</u> a one-ton car can readily triumph over a half-ton <u>moose</u>, it's a Pyrrhic victory. As one Alaskan biologist puts it: "You've seen the damage an ordinary white-tailed deer can do to a car? You should see what a bull <u>moose</u> can do!"

> John Madson, "The North Woods: A Horn of Plenty
> for Old Bucketnose," *Smithsonian,* July 1986: 104.

A.   The custom of the birthday cake began during the thirteenth century in Germany, part of a day-long celebration called *Kinderfest*—or "child festival"—marking the birthday of a child. *Kinderfest* began at dawn when a child was awakened by the arrival of a cake topped with lighted candles. The one candle more than the total of the child's years represented the "light of life." The candles were burned and replaced all day until the cake was eaten after dinner. At this time the child made a wish and blew out the candles. The candles had to be extinguished with a single breath. For the wish to come true, it had to remain a secret.

> Adapted from Charles Panati, *Extraordinary Origins
> of Everyday Things* (New York: Harper, 1987), 33.

1.   Good reading, therefore, though it is not essentially an affectional or moral or intellectual activity, has something in common with all three. In love we escape from our self into one another. In the moral

sphere, every act of justice or charity involves putting ourselves in the other person's place and thus transcending our own competitive particularity. In coming to understand anything, we are rejecting the facts as they are for us in favour of the facts as they are. The primary impulse of each is to maintain and aggrandise himself. The secondary impulse is to go out of the self, to correct its provincialism and heal its loneliness. In love, in virtue, in the pursuit of the arts, we are doing just this.

C. S. Lewis, *An Experiment in Criticism* (London: Cambridge University Press, 1961), 138.

12.5   PARAGRAPH DIVISION

Directions: Divide each of the following passages into paragraphs by inserting the ¶ sign where a new paragraph should begin.

A.   American mythology makes common cause with another formidable force: American complacency. Harold Stevenson's work in 1979–1980 with children, mothers, and teachers from three countries suggests the problem by contrasting performance and attitudes. In one statistical he rated the mathematics achievement of equal numbers of students from Japan, Taiwan, and the United States. Among the top 100 first-graders there were only fifteen American children. Almost unbelievably, among the top 100 fifth-graders there was only one American child. In contrast, among the bottom 100 first-graders, fifty-eight were American, and among the bottom 100 fifth-graders, sixty-seven were American. There was more. The shocker came in the attitude surveys. More than 40 percent of the American mothers were "very satisfied" with how their children were doing in school, whereas less than 5 percent of the Japanese and Chinese mothers were "very satisfied." Nearly a third of the Chinese and Japanese mothers said they were "not satisfied" with their children's performance, but only 10 percent of the American mothers expressed dissatisfaction. The jarring enthusiasm of the Americans persisted when it came to attitudes toward the quality of the schools themselves. Ninety-one percent judged that the school was doing an "excellent" or "good" job. Only 42 percent of the Chinese mothers and 39 percent of the Japanese mothers were this positive.

> Michael J. Barrett, "The Case for More School
> Days," *The Atlantic*, November 1990: 94.

1.   The Civil War is, for the American imagination, the great single event of our history. Without too much wrenching, it may, in fact, be said to *be* American history. Before the Civil War we had no history in the deepest and most inward sense. There was, of course, the noble vision of the Founding Fathers articulated in the Declaration and the Constitution—the dream of freedom incarnated in a more perfect union. But the Revolution did not create a nation except on paper; and too often in the

following years the vision of the Founding Fathers, which men had suffered and died to validate, became merely a daydream of easy and automatic victories, a vulgar delusion of manifest destiny, a conviction of being a people divinely chosen to live on milk and honey at small expense. The vision had not been finally submitted to the test of history. There was little awareness of the cost of having a history. The anguished scrutiny of the meaning of the vision in experience had not become a national reality. It became a reality, and we became a nation, only with the Civil War. The Civil War is our only "felt" history—history lived in the national imagination. This is not to say that the War is always, and by all men, felt the same way. Quite the contrary. But this fact is an index to the very complexity, depth, and fundamental significance of the event. It is an overwhelming and vital image of human, and national, experience.

Robert Penn Warren, *The Legacy of the Civil War* (Cambridge, MA: Harvard University Press, 1961), 3–4.

13.1   COMBINING SENTENCES—SET 1

Directions: Rewrite each of the following groups of sentences as one sentence by using a coordinating or subordinating conjunction or a transitional expression. Make sure that your new sentences are correctly punctuated and that you have made any necessary verb tense changes.

Example:

Original sentences: I don't know whose car hit mine. I noticed green paint streaks on its doors.

Revision: I don't know whose car hit mine, but I did notice green paint streaks on its doors.

A. Rupert hasn't turned in a single paper this semester. He hasn't turned in a piece of homework.

B. Death Valley is the lowest place in the United States. It is also the hottest place.

C. Many television stations in the United States are on the air twenty-four hours a day. In many foreign countries the number of broadcasting hours is carefully regulated.

D. Robert and Annie have been separated for two years. They have been meeting recently to try to reconcile.

E. We recommended the latest exhibit at the Cartoon Art Museum to our cousins. We knew how much they enjoyed political humor.

1. John F. Kennedy was president for less than three years. He was one of our most admired presidents.

2. Jules knocked on the door for a few minutes. The music kept blaring inside.

3. January 27 was Mozart's birthday. The classical radio station played only Mozart's music on that day.

4. Representative Danehy strongly supports citizens' rights to privacy. She introduced a bill prohibiting companies from gathering information about customers without their express consent.

5. We tried everything to get the chewing gum out of the carpet. We froze it with an ice cube, we poured nail polish remover on it, and we even applied some peanut butter.

13.2 COMBINING SENTENCES—SET 2

Directions: Edit the following paragraphs, using coordination, subordination, and transitions to make the sentences more readable. See example in 13.1 Combining Sentences—Set 1.

A.   Two literary works captured the hysteria of the Salem witch hunts. The works were written over a century apart. Nathaniel Hawthorne wrote the story "Young Goodman Brown" in 1835. Hawthorne's great-great-grandfather Colonel John Hathorne was one of the magistrates who had tried those accused of witchcraft. Arthur Miller wrote the play *The Crucible* in 1953. Hawthorne and Miller set their works in 1692 Salem. They used as characters some of the real people who had been afflicted and accused. Miller wrote his play at the time of another witch hunt. This witch hunt was directed against alleged Communists in the U.S. government. It was also directed at alleged Communists in the arts and entertainment worlds. No one was hanged in the 1950s. Many lives were destroyed. Many careers were ended prematurely.

1.   Salem, Massachusetts, was a quiet town in 1692. In February of that year, several teenage girls began having odd symptoms. These symptoms included wailing, thrashing about, seeing visions, and feeling physical sensations. They said that they felt as if they were being pinched or bitten. One of the afflicted girls was the daughter of the village pastor, Reverend Samuel Parris. Other girls were daughters of village families. Some girls were servants in village households. The girls accused some village women and servants of tormenting them. They accused some men also. They even accused a child. The accused were brought before the court for examinations and trials. They were sent to prison in neighboring towns and in Boston. By September, nineteen of the convicted had been hanged. One man had been slowly crushed to death. By April 1693, the witchcraft hysteria was over.

13.3   EXPANDING SENTENCES

Directions: Expand each of the following sentences by using one of the seven ways to add details discussed in the text (adding individual modifiers, prepositional phrases, absolute phrases, participial phrases, infinitive phrases, subordinate clauses, or relative clauses). Then name the method that you used.

Example:

Original sentence: Eli unlocked the front door.

Expanded sentence: Peering nervously around the corner, Eli unlocked the front door.

Method of expanding sentence: _participial phrase_

A.   Mr. Stevenson planted bamboo in the front yard.

B.   Bruce mailed his mortgage payment.

C.   Sam emerged from the swimming hole.

D.   Juanita was busy talking on the phone.

E.   Doris declared that she'd had a hard day at work.

1.   Quilting is a popular hobby again today.

2.   Bob bought a hybrid car.

3.   Jane Smith won the bake-off.

4.   Grandfather appeared at our front door.

5.   James wears lifts in his shoes.

13.4 USING ACTIVE AND PASSIVE VOICE

Directions: Rewrite each of the following sentences, changing it from passive to active voice.

Example:

Original sentence: The Thanksgiving dinner for the homeless was cooked by neighborhood volunteers.

Revision: Neighborhood volunteers cooked the Thanksgiving dinner for the homeless.

A. The cellist was given a standing ovation by the audience when she finished her solo.

B. Many recyclable materials have been diverted from the waste stream by diligent recyclers.

C. Harsh conditions are endured by sled dogs carrying medical supplies to snowed-in Alaskan villages.

D. Freud's identification of the ego, the id, and the superego as the components of personality has been disputed by modern psychoanalysts.

E. The blood samples have been tested for their DNA content by the lab technicians.

1. The French army under Philip VI was defeated by English archers at the Battle of Crécy, the first important battle of the Hundred Years' War.

2. Maple syrup was produced by Native Americans long before French and Indian explorers came to North America.

3. The buzzer was pressed repeatedly by the sweaty game-show contestant, but the question was answered by another contestant first.

4. The dark cavern was entered by a search party carrying flashlights.

5. The presence of water on the moon has been revealed by satellite photographs.

13.5   USING STRONG, EFFECTIVE CONSTRUCTIONS

Directions: Revise each of the following sentences by editing the nominal constructions, use of expletives, or negative constructions.

Example:

Original sentence: The architect gave a description of his plans for the kitchen renovation.

Revision: The architect described his plans for the kitchen renovation.

A.   It is essential for you to put the trash out early on Monday mornings.

B.   Our physics instructor never not let us turn in our work late if we had a good excuse for doing so.

C.   There is strong evidence that indicates that people are affected by second-hand smoke.

D.   The sales representative gave a demonstration to show how the new printer could produce high-quality photographs.

E.   The neighborhood watch group conducted a vote to ask that the city assign more police patrols to this area after midnight.

1.   There is a city law that prohibits bicyclists from riding on the sidewalk.

2.   It is not uncommon for residents of Northern California to experience earth tremors.

3.   The committee had a review of the proposals for the new roadway.

4.   That song is not unlike the others on the band's previous albums.

5.   We had a preference for taking an early flight in order that we could arrive at our destination alert and refreshed.

13.6   USING PARALLEL STRUCTURE

Directions: Revise each of the following sentences to correct the errors in parallel structure.

Example:

Original sentence: Their new home is spacious, well lit, and it has good insulation.

Revision: Their new home is spacious, well lit, and well insulated.

A. Americans invented jazz as well as developing rock and roll.

B. Soft contact lenses must be washed daily and cleaned with a special solution, and you must store them carefully.

C. To be comfortable at the campsite, they wanted not only to be able to light a decent fire, but having access to an electrical hookup would be desirable, too.

D. Listening to the birds chirping in the country is better than to be bombarded by traffic noise when you are in the city.

E. Denise enjoys running, knitting, and she collects stuffed animals.

1. We couldn't decide whether to walk to the movie or if taking a cab would be better.

2. Several proven ways to relieve stress are massage, meditation, and exercising regularly.

3. When the play finished its run on Broadway, the lead actor said he was tired but that he was pleased with his performance.

4. Annoyed at the long checkout line, the shopper began to sigh loudly, tapping his foot, and glance at his watch.

5. At college Lucy discovered that she enjoyed living in the dormitory, new friends, and economics.

13.7   DIVIDING RAMBLING SENTENCES

Directions: Rewrite each of the following rambling sentences to correct the excessive coordination.

Example:

Original sentence: The CDC is a federal agency that has the responsibility for tracing the sources of infectious diseases, and it is also responsible for diagnosing infectious diseases, and it is located in Atlanta.

Revision: The CDC, a federal agency located in Atlanta, is responsible for tracing the sources of and diagnosing infectious diseases.

A.   Sunspots were discovered in the eighteenth century, and they have remained a mystery for two centuries, but now scientists are beginning to understand these solar phenomena.

B.   Millions of American teenagers take the SAT today, but this test was not developed until 1926, and it was not widely used until 1943.

C.   Video games are big business, and much of their popularity is due to increasingly sophisticated graphics, but the best-selling video game in history is still the hand-held Game Boy.

D.   Mars has channel-like features, and they have intrigued generations of scientists, and more recently they have helped stimulate a search for water on the red planet.

E.   The water cascaded over the falls, and we watched the salmon leaping into the air, and we wondered what compelled them to such struggle.

1.   The great masterpiece of Japanese literature is *The Tale of Genji*, and it was written during the Heian period (794–1185) by Lady Murasaki Shikibu; it was not translated into English until the twentieth century.

2.   Conventional diets limit the amount of fat and increase the amount of carbohydrates, but high-protein diets are becoming popular, and many people are making bacon, steak, and butter part of their weight-loss plan.

3.   Lake Nicaragua was cut off from the Pacific Ocean by lava; it is ninety-six miles long and thirty-nine miles wide, and it is the only freshwater lake in the world to contain people-eating sharks.

4.   Old-fashioned fairy tales were frightening, and they were intended to be, and children heard them and were likely to stay near home or on the path in the woods, so the stories taught safety.

5.   Internet companies are starting up at a record pace, and every type of business has been affected, but a shortage of qualified workers, office space, and advertising makes their success far from certain.

13.8 VARYING SENTENCE STRUCTURE

Directions: Rewrite each of the following loose sentences as a periodic sentence.

Example:

Loose sentence: Neil Armstrong was the first person to set foot on the moon.

Periodic sentence: The first person to set foot on the moon was Neil Armstrong.

A. A tropical storm is called a hurricane when its wind speeds exceed seventy-five miles per hour.

B. Grits did not become common in the South until after the Civil War even though they are now a staple of southern cuisine.

C. Today many cartoons are designed for adult viewers, although some people still associate animation with children.

D. Charles Dickens's *A Christmas Carol* sold more than six thousand copies, largely because of its author's popularity.

E. The liver is an irreplaceable organ of the body because machines cannot duplicate its various and highly complex functions.

1. Geographic regions of the United States may experience severe financial distress before the nation as a whole meets the established criteria for a recession.

2. You need to get estimates from several suppliers if you want the best possible price.

3. Ancient Rome was the first society governed by a bicameral legislature.

4. Southeastern Oregon is largely unpopulated because it is a harsh, alkaline desert.

5. Every stamp collector wants a 1928 Graf Zeppelin stamp because it is very rare.

14.1 SELECTING EXACT WORDS

Directions: Revise each of the following sentences to eliminate clichés, pretentious language, flowery phrases, and slang.

Example: My boyfriend thought that movie was ~~the pits~~. *disgusting*

A.   Beyond a shadow of a doubt, *Blow-Up* is Antonioni's masterpiece.

B.   Most of the money from the fundraiser went to support the economically disadvantaged in their time of need.

C.   Severe diminution of precipitation and greatly elevated temperatures are threatening the corn crop.

D.   Honest lawyers who charge fair rates are few and far between.

E.   San Francisco, a city that has twice rebuilt after suffering the devastating effects of two earthquakes, is living proof that every cloud has a silver lining.

1.   The president was bent out of shape by the constant threats to the peacekeeping forces.

2.   Enlistment in the military grew by leaps and bounds during the first few weeks of World War II.

3.   The coach tried to get the football players psyched for the Homecoming game.

4.   Midwestern summers are hot and humid from the crack of dawn until the dead of night.

5.   Optimizing its opportunities for profit maximization, the board of directors voted to sell the patent for the medical device.

14.2   CUTTING WORDINESS

Directions: Edit each of the following sentences to eliminate deadwood, redundancy, and unnecessary modifiers.

Example: Some ~~new~~ beginners attended the yoga class.

A.   Most eye-catching advertisements in magazines attract the reader's attention with designs that are bold and colors that are bright.

B.   Combine nutmeg, cinnamon, salt, and flour together and then stir the mixture of the ingredients for five minutes.

C.   An ovenbird is an American bird that is a member of the warbler family and that builds a nest that resembles an oven on the floor of a forest.

D.   We watched anxiously as the climbers descended down into the ravine; soon they were no longer visible to the naked eye.

E.   Many municipalities have begun to initiate recycling programs due to the fact that their landfills are filled to capacity with solid waste.

1.   The popular movie *Gone with the Wind* is a well-loved film that is based on a novel by Margaret Mitchell.

2.   Train service to Dublin-Pleasanton will resume again after the end of the transit strike.

3.   The professor was impressed by Sean's very unique solution to the physics problem.

4.   There is strong resistance to using corporal punishment on the part of many child psychologists.

5.   It has been shown that the duration of the common cold can be reduced by giving the person who has the cold doses of zinc glutonate in the form of lozenges.

14.3   EDITING PHRASES AND CLAUSES

Directions: Edit each of the following sentences by trimming unnecessary wording in phrases and clauses.

Example:

Original sentence: We were aware of the fact that these streets could be dangerous after dark.

Revision: We knew that these streets could be dangerous after dark.

A.   The cuisine of the Mediterranean region of the world features a varied mixture of different kinds of foods from southern Europe and the Islamic part of the world.

B.   Beginning in the 1930s and continuing to the present day, writers have often been interested in using Hollywood as a setting for their novels.

C.   There are usually research assistants at major universities to help and assist professors to conduct a large number of research projects.

D.   Simón Bolívar is considered by many people to be a hero because of his work in helping to defeat, through armed conflict, the Spanish armies in South America.

E.   Old-growth forests are forests that are at least two hundred years old and that have never been cut.

1.   It was William Harvey who first wrote about the circulation of the blood.

2.   At this point in time, citizens are more aware of political corruption than they were before the Watergate scandal.

3.   In terms of its land size, Canada is considered to be the second-largest country in the world.

4.   Traditional zoos are considered by most authorities to be detrimental to animals due to the fact that they deny animals truly natural conditions in which they can live.

5.   Companies that want to sell their products to television viewers often bombard these viewers with repeated advertisements played at a very loud volume.

14.4 DEVELOPING AN ACADEMIC STYLE

Directions: Revise each of the following sentences to reflect an academic style. Make sure that each has an appropriate level of formality; uses personal pronouns sparingly; and does not contain jargon, technical terms, or unnecessary qualifiers.

eliminated

Example: Double-check the stack of ~~foul~~ pages before you submit the final review package.

A.   I absolutely agree with your assessment that the president has way too much power.

B.   Ernest bought Honda's new crossover that was fully loaded with power steering, dual suspension, and anti-lock brakes.

C.   One does not always recognize one's limitations when one is young.

D.   American farmers sometimes get stuck with genetically modified crops because European markets won't buy them.

E.   The new patient in the ICU sustained internal injuries as well as contusions and abrasions when he fell from a second-story window.

1.   In my opinion, students shouldn't have to take a proficiency exam in order to graduate from high school.

2.   The supervisor interfaced with each department head before the sales conference.

3.   We felt gypped because we couldn't get into the lecture, but we were used to that sort of thing.

4.   The instructions for assembling the CPU were user friendly.

5.   Many of the problems that southerners experience in the North, to which I can attest from my own personal experience, stem from language differences.

14.5   Using Fair, Respectful Language

Directions: Edit each of the following sentences to eliminate any terms that reflect bias toward gender, race, disabilities, impairment, age, or ethnicity.

human beings

Example: Global warming affects all ~~of mankind~~.

A.   Off-duty policemen sometimes encounter crimes in progress.

B.   Maurice has been confined to a wheelchair since his diving accident.

C.   My mother was a typical suburban housewife before she started law school.

D.   The nation's forefathers created the Declaration of Independence and the Bill of Rights to define the rights of American citizens.

E.   Senator Mona Morrison, wearing a light blue pantsuit and a tasteful string of pearls, and Representative Tom Robinson addressed the rally.

1.   A nurse who works the night shift must have a supportive husband and family.

2.   The benefit successfully raised funds for victims of AIDS.

3.   All of the cargo ships were manned by well-trained recruits.

4.   We were pleased to discover the variety of Oriental restaurants in our new neighborhood.

5.   The Americans with Disabilities Act guarantees that the handicapped have equal access to public buildings.

15.1   USING THE CORRECT WORD—SET 1

Directions: In each of the following sentences, box the correct word in the parentheses that best completes the sentence.

Example: Learning a foreign language takes (| a lot | , alot, allot) of effort.

A.   Kate did not feel (good, well) after eating the shrimp salad.

B.   Surprisingly, the tour bus remained (stationary, stationery) during the earth tremors.

C.   You're not (suppose to, supposed to) open your presents until Christmas morning.

D.   The dog (who, that) belongs to the neighbors usually sleeps in our backyard.

E.   Conscientious campers (try to, try and) find safe, wind-free places to build cooking fires.

1.   Unshaven and red-eyed, the newspaper editor looked (as if, like) he had worked for days without sleep.

2.   Distribute the winnings (between, among) the three remaining candidates.

3.   We were (all ready, already) in the car when Homer decided to return to the house for a map.

4.   (Less, Fewer) than half of the presidents of the United States were born outside the original thirteen colonies.

5.   The officer directing traffic told us to (precede, proceed) with caution through the construction area.

15.2 USING THE CORRECT WORD—SET 2

Directions: In each of the following sentences, box the correct word contained in the parentheses that best completes the sentence.

Example: For the coffee merchant, inhaling the aroma of the roasting Colombian beans was a (| sensuous |, sensual) pleasure.

A. Some forms of Hindu religion maintain that the physical world is an (allusion, illusion).

B. Austin is the (capital, capitol) of Texas.

C. The representative who had taken bribes was (censered, censored, censured) by his peers.

D. The purple velour couch (complimented, complemented) the navy shag rug and the bluish-gray abstract painting.

E. Mitsuko's father was an (eminent, imminent) Asian art historian.

1. We (waited for, waited on) you at the doctor's office for more than an hour.

2. The (amount, number) of books in Fran's library is truly impressive.

3. Pollen in the air can (affect, effect) people's allergies.

4. LaVonne placed the antique coins in (discreet, discrete) containers for the auction preview.

5. Most people in America either (emigrated, immigrated) from another country or descended from someone who (emigrated, immigrated) to this one.

PART 5
GRAMMAR

19.1 IDENTIFYING NOUNS

Directions: Underline the nouns in the following sentences.

Example: <u>E-mail</u> allows computer <u>users</u> to communicate with other <u>people</u> all over the <u>world</u>.

A. Some critics believe that people who watch too much television have short attention spans.

B. A general encyclopedia is a collection of knowledge and information on a broad range of topics.

C. Early in the twentieth century two hundred button factories in the United States almost depleted the supply of freshwater mussels.

D. In 1988, divers off the coast of Turkey found jars of baked clay dating from the thirteenth century B.C.

E. Hikers in Yellowstone National Park are advised to wear layers of clothing and to carry a good supply of water.

1. The picture of A. B. Peterson, who wrote the words to "Waltzing Matilda," appears on Australia's ten-dollar bill.

2. The introduction of DVD players into the home video market has greatly impacted the rental of VHS tapes.

3. Babies born at sea level usually weigh more than babies born at higher altitudes.

4. For many years the Empire State Building was the tallest building in the world.

5. Standards of beauty vary greatly from country to country.

19.2   IDENTIFYING PRONOUNS AND ANTECEDENTS

Directions: Underline the pronouns in the following sentences. If a pronoun has an antecedent, box the antecedent and draw an arrow from the underlined pronoun to the antecedent.

Example: She herself intends to represent those clients.

A.   Nobody spoke against the proposal, but each of us had reasons to object to it.

B.   The football players congratulated themselves for playing a great game and waved to all of their cheering fans in the bleachers.

C.   Most of the nation's small businesses are quite concerned about the rising costs of their employees' health insurance.

D.   These are the files that you should return to their original locations.

E.   People who live in that part of the country are used to those extreme temperatures.

1.   Signaling to those who steadied her ladder, the firefighter began her long descent into the burning house.

2.   The grass, which is already turning brown, will die if it doesn't rain soon.

3.   The two dogs growled at each other; then one began to show its teeth and moved closer to me.

4.   My brother and sister arrived unexpectedly; I hadn't seen them in almost a year.

5.   Everyone in the room heard the loud noise, but no one could identify it.

19.3 FORMS OF PERSONAL PRONOUNS

Directions: In the following sentences, box the correct pronoun form contained in the parentheses. Make sure that the pronoun agrees with its antecedent.

Example: Matilda gave the present to Mary and (I, me).

A.   Fred and (myself, me, I) will show you to your seat.

B.   Everyone should bring (their, his or her, his) own sleeping bag for the camping trip.

C.   The best players on the team—George, Emil, and (me, I)—were elected co-captains.

D.   To (who, whom) was the president referring in his speech?

E.   Either my father or your uncle is going on the trip, so (they, he) will have to bring proof of

identification.

1.   John wants to show the visiting ambassador and (me, I) the museum.

2.   Many of (us, we) racing fans were cheering as the horse crossed the finish line.

3.   That must be (her, she) pounding on the front door.

4.   (Who, whom) did you see peering out of the shadows?

5.   Each of the girl scouts was responsible for (their, her) own cookie sales.

19.4   USING RELATIVE PRONOUNS IN RELATIVE AND NOUN CLAUSES

Directions: Box the correct pronoun form contained in the parentheses, underline the relative/adjective or noun clause, and explain what role the boxed pronoun plays in the relative or noun clause and what role the clause plays in the complete sentence.

Example: Tell me (who , whom) is coming for dinner.

Explanation: *Who* is the subject of the noun clause *who is coming to dinner,* which is the direct object of the verb *tell* in the complete sentence.

A.   (Whoever, whomever) you help with the homework will be grateful.

B.   I will speak with (whoever, whomever) answers the phone.

C.   Denise rewarded the boy (who, whom) found and returned her wallet.

D.   Aunt Tillie was the only person (whom, who) the frightened children trusted.

E.   The Spanish explorers (who, whom) followed Columbus to the Caribbean discovered small amounts

of gold as well as fierce resistance by the Caribs, a warlike tribe.

1.   All afternoon Carlos looked for the woman (who, whom) he had seen at the dance the night before.

2.   I know someone (who, whom) exceeded her limits on four credit cards.

3.   Give this book to (whoever, whomever) wants it.

4.   I asked to speak with the manager (who, whom) was in charge of customer service.

5.   The villagers (who, whom) the earthquake displaced are now refugees in Europe.

20.1   CLASSES OF VERBS

Directions: In the following sentences label the simple subject **S**; then underline the complete verb and label it **AV** (active verb) or **LV** (linking verb). If the active verb has a direct object, label it **DO**. If the linking verb has a predicate nominative (**PN**) or predicate adjective (**PA**), label that word.

$$\overset{S}{}\quad\overset{AV}{}\quad\overset{DO}{}$$

Example: Many commuters <u>ride</u> the subway every day.

A.   Mary was writing her term paper all night.

B.   Some of the voters wondered about the election results.

C.   The winner was the candidate with slightly more than a third of the votes.

D.   His alibi sounded mighty suspicious.

E.   I have owned this Honda for seventeen years.

1.   There are some strange vegetables in my soup.

2.   The embezzler was not the best person for the bookkeeping job.

3.   Willie had grown tall over the summer.

4.   The realtors have been showing this property to prospective buyers for months.

5.   The organic farmers grew baby spinach for the local markets.

20.2   FORMS OF VERBS

Directions: In each of the following sentences, write the correct form of the verb contained in the parentheses in the blank. Consider the context of the sentence carefully when selecting the best verb form to complete the sentence.

Example: The sun (set) <u>will set</u> this evening at 6:30 p.m.

A.   Scientists have only just (begin) _____ to unlock the secrets of human DNA.

B.   Many soldiers who (fight) _____ in the first Gulf War experience recurring

nightmares.

C.   Two centuries ago huge flocks of Carolina parakeets (darken) _____ the skies all

along the East Coast.

D.   Many Ice Age animals (freeze) _____ when they were trapped by avalanches in

mountainous areas.

E.   We already (watch) _____ that movie twice on TV during the past week.

1.   I (run) _____ away quickly to get away from those hornets.

2.   Kerry (leave) _____ this package here for you yesterday.

3.   Vitamins and food supplements (suppose) _____ to cure many common ailments.

4.   Harriet (go) _____ to Italy last year to view Renaissance paintings.

5.   The runner (know) _____ as the fastest member of the team.

20.3   SEQUENCE OF VERB TENSES—SET 1

Directions: Correct the errors in verb forms and tenses in the following sentences so that they have the correct sequence of verb tenses. If a sentence is correct, write "Correct."

Example: I ~~ran~~ *was running* across the street when my shoelace broke.

A.   The term *tailgate trombone* once referred to a New Orleans trombonist who plays while standing on the back of a horse-drawn parade cart.

B.   The president was talking for an hour and a half now, and he still hasn't told us anything new.

C.   When this new policy goes into effect, our titles will be different, our office locations will change, and our responsibilities will increase.

D.   People climbed Mt. Washington for more than one hundred years, but no one fell from that ravine before yesterday.

E.   The *Mahabharata*, which was written in India around 200 B.C., contained about 3,000,000 words.

1.   Fossil remains found in Antarctica had linked that continent with South America and have provided further evidence that the two landmasses were once connected.

2.   Because he cheated on the exam, Donald failed the course.

3.   Primitive people assumed that a toothache was a sign that some god was angry with them.

4.   I see Lois from across the room an hour ago, but she still doesn't recognize me.

5.   Elephant herds haul away tons of silt from shallow water holes after their ritualistic herd baths; thus, they cleaned the water and created water holes for other animals.

20.4   SEQUENCE OF VERB TENSES—SET 2

Directions: Correct the errors in verb forms and tenses in the following sentences so that they have the correct sequence of verb tenses. If there are no verb errors in a sentence, write "Correct."

Example: Be sure that you have locked the door securely before you ~~will~~ leave the house.

A.   After the tsunami destroyed Marcel's house, he received a check from his insurance company.

B.   In the not-too-distant future, it may be possible for people to grow new organs that will be replacing old ones.

C.   Offshore tornadoes, which are called *waterspouts*, were known to drop large numbers of fish on inland communities from time to time.

D.   *Letters from the Earth*, which Mark Twain wrote toward the end of his life, revealed his deep pessimism about the human race.

E.   We will be waiting for you in the hotel lobby when you arrive.

1.   Most scientists believe that greenhouse gases are destroying the ozone layer; however, some others are disagreeing.

2.   Physicians on the American frontier provided various services: they set broken bones, had delivered babies, pulled teeth, and inspected water supplies.

3.   Rosalind has weeded the garden for hours, but she still has plenty of work left to do before sunset.

4.   If I knew Francine's boyfriend was a sumo wrestler, I wouldn't have asked her for a date.

5.   Battles were once fought with swords and maces, which were used to crush armor.

20.5 ACTIVE AND PASSIVE VOICE

Directions: Rewrite the following sentences, changing the verb or verbs from passive to active voice. If the passive voice is necessary in the sentence, just write "Correct."

Example:

Original sentence: Malaria, a debilitating and sometimes fatal disease, can be cured by doctors.

Revision: Doctors can cure malaria, a debilitating and sometimes fatal disease.

A.   Unattended luggage is viewed very suspiciously by security officials at airports.

B.   The well had been mysteriously poisoned, so the farmers were forced to leave their land.

C.   More than one thousand people lost their lives when the *Lusitania*, a British steamer, was torpedoed by a German submarine on May 7, 1915.

D.   Potential jurors were asked by the defense attorney to state their opinions on the death penalty.

E.   Taxes must be paid on winnings by television contestants who obtain large cash prizes.

1.   As much as 400 inches of rain per year is received by some Hawaiian islands per year.

2.   This package with no return address was left on our doorstep last night.

3.   The cats were fed by our neighbor while we were vacationing in Mexico.

4.   Plimoth Plantation, a re-creation of the Pilgrims' first settlement in America, is visited by thousands of tourists each year.

5.   The first telephone conversation was held between Alexander Graham Bell and Thomas A. Watson on March 10, 1876.

20.6   MOOD OF A VERB

Directions: Edit the following sentences to make the verb use correct. If the sentence is correctly written, write "Correct."

                                                  were
Example: If I ~~was~~ the instructor, I wouldn't assign so much homework.

A.   The principal demanded that we brought a note from our parents to explain our absences.

B.   George will be very angry if he finds out that we went to the beach without him.

C.   If the workers voted today, they will not be able to agree on a settlement with management.

D.   Marianne wishes that she went to Paris before starting college.

E.   The landlord insisted that we should stop playing the stereo at full volume.

1.   If I was living in a warmer climate right now, I wouldn't have to pay such exorbitant heating bills.

2.   If Henry gets a promotion, he would move to a bigger apartment.

3.   I wouldn't live in a big city even if I would have the chance to do so.

4.   Would you trade your SUV for a smaller vehicle if you did not have enough money to fill it with gas each week?

5.   It's not too late to insist that our visitors would stay until the fog lifts.

20.7   IRREGULAR VERBS

Directions: In each of the following sentences, box the correct verb form contained within the parentheses.

Example: After being read his rights, the murder suspect was (lead, ☐led☐) to a holding cell.

A.   The tourists (lay, laid) on the Brazilian beach for hours listening to the pounding surf.

B.   The Gilbert Stuart portraits of George and Martha Washington were (hung, hanged) in the Boston Athenaeum.

C.   According to Homer's *Iliad*, Achilles (dragged, drug) Hector's corpse behind his chariot.

D.   Mother had (set, sat) the package on the table before going out for the evening.

E.   The racing team (raised, rose) the yacht's sail and turned it into the wind.

1.   The frightened children had (lain, laid) awake all night after hearing the ghost stories.

2.   Calling repeatedly for help, the desperate sailor had (swam, swum) in circles for hours before being rescued.

3.   During the hurricane the coastal roads had been (tore, torn) up by huge waves and fierce winds.

4.   The nervous job applicant (set, sat) on the edge of her chair during the interview.

5.   By the end of the party, we had (drank, drunk) every beverage in the house.

20.8 VERBALS

Directions: Edit each of the following sentences so that it contains the correct form of the gerund, infinitive, past participle, or present participle. Then identify the type of verbal used and explain its function in the sentence.

to receive

Example: George did not expect ~~receiving~~ a letter from Louis.

infinitive—direct object

A. The statistics on the prevalence of underage drinking and driving are very depressed.

  _____

B. Nancy finished to study her homework once her friends left.

  _____

C. All her adult life my grandmother has avoided to eat raisins because she was forced to eat them

  during the Depression.

  _____

D. The surprising look on the faces of the winners indicated that they had not realized the effectiveness

  of their performance.

  _____

E. The bossy older sister enjoyed to make her timid younger sister do all the housecleaning.

  _____

1. The pilot ordered the passengers turning off their cell phones for the rest of the flight.

  _____

2. The stunning family received the shocked news without comment.

  _____

3. The committee discussed to adopt the proposal but postponed voting on it until the next meeting.

  _____

4.   Marisa's grandfather told a fascinated story about his life in the circus.

   _____

5.   On her first trip to Iceland, Hortense could not imagine to be in a colder place.

   _____

21.1   IDENTIFYING ADJECTIVES (PROPER, PREDICATE)

Directions: In each of the following sentences, underline each adjective (including articles) and box the word that it modifies. Draw an arrow from the adjective to the word that it modifies.

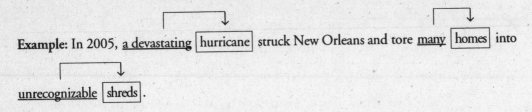

Example: In 2005, <u>a devastating</u> | hurricane | struck New Orleans and tore <u>many</u> | homes | into

<u>unrecognizable</u> | shreds | .

A.   In some national parks the movements of grizzly bears wearing electronic collars are tracked by satellite.

B.   Every year numerous bicyclists compete in the grueling Tour de France, hoping to win the yellow jersey.

C.   The semiprecious stones known as garnets may be red, green, yellow, or white.

D.   Susan's allergic reaction was caused by the great amounts of pollen in the air and the heavy humidity.

E.   British and American words with the same meanings can vary slightly in their spellings.

1.   My older brother found a feral cat in the neighbor's yard yesterday.

2.   Although the plot was familiar, the new film was better than we had expected because of the fine acting.

3.   Some specialists in foreign languages find permanent employment in the diplomatic corps or in international business.

4.   A professional photographer's shots of world-famous celebrities often become collector's items.

5.   The visiting relatives said that the best part of their trip was dining at the expensive French restaurant.

21.2 IDENTIFYING ADVERBS AND THE ROLES THEY PLAY

Directions: In the following sentences, underline each adverb and box the word that it modifies. Next, draw an arrow from the adverb to the boxed word. Then label the boxed word as a verb, an adjective, or an adverb.

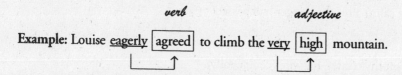

Example: Louise eagerly agreed to climb the very high mountain.

A.   Fred answered the questions slowly and reluctantly since he had not read the assignment.

B.   Physicists have often speculated—and have almost always disagreed—about the size of the universe.

C.   Service at this lovely restaurant sometimes involves a longer wait because entrees must be individually prepared.

D.   That is the most disgusting thing I have ever heard!

E.   If you submit your essay tomorrow, it will be too late to receive a passing grade.

1.   The largest diamonds are seldom the clearest and occasionally are the most roughly cut.

2.   California is well known for its earthquakes, and Easterners who have moved there are usually fearful of them.

3.   While he was carefully examining the walls of the ancient building, the archaeologist suddenly discovered a small cache of coins that were easily two thousand years old.

4.   As the airplane gradually descended through the threatening dark clouds, the pilot glanced quickly at the rapidly falling fuel gauge.

5.   In the middle of an exquisitely graceful performance, the figure skater suddenly lurched forward and then fell heavily to the ice.

21.3   FORMS OF ADJECTIVES AND ADVERBS

Directions: In each of the following sentences, box the correct comparative or superlative form of the adjective or adverb contained in the parentheses.

Example: Irene was (calmer , more calm) after the danger had passed.

A.   After their long separation, Timothy treated his wife (cool, coolly).

B.   Yolanda felt (bad, badly) when she woke up this morning, but now she feels (worse, worst).

C.   Because the road was icy, Fred drove home (slower, more slowly) than he usually did.

D.   I voted for Mindy because she is the (more, most) qualified of the three candidates.

E.   Dominic spoke very (reasonable, reasonably); he didn't lose his temper once.

1.   Your Halloween mask looks (scarier, more scary) than mine does.

2.   Now that she has new running shoes, Josie can get to work (quicker, more quickly) than I can.

3.   Which falls is the (higher, highest) in the world, Yosemite Falls or Angel Falls?

4.   John was the (better, best) blocker on the team while Fernando was the (better, best) of the two

place kickers.

5.   His muscles developed so (good, well) that soon Bill was the (stronger, strongest) kid in the

neighborhood.

21.4   Correct Use of Adjectives and Adverbs

Directions: Correct any errors in adjective or adverb use in the following sentences. If a sentence has no errors, write "Correct."

directly
Example: Please ship the package ~~direct~~ to my house.

A.   We all felt badly because Helen didn't win first prize.

B.   Carlo's solution to the math problem was very unique.

C.   If you're not real sick, you'll have to take the exam.

D.   Colonel Smith was the most decorated of the thirty veterans.

E.   Karen looked sickly for the first time in years, but the color of her complexion improved quick.

1.   I don't like that instructor because he doesn't grade fair.

2.   My date acted so obnoxious that we had to leave the party early.

3.   While approaching her parked car on the dark street, the woman looked slow behind herself and then began to walk rapid.

4.   Omar sang so good that the audience considered him the best of the five performers.

5.   Because my mother disconnected the refrigerator by mistake yesterday, the meat smells terribly.

21.5   PREPOSITIONS AND PREPOSITIONAL PHRASES

Directions: In the following sentences, enclose each prepositional phrase in parentheses, label the preposition **P** and the object(s) of the preposition **OP**, and underline the word or words that the prepositional phrase modifies.

$$P \qquad OP$$

Example: The fans <u>were sitting</u> (in the bleachers).

A.   Legends about vampires are found in many cultures throughout the world.

B.   In most legends vampires leave their graves at night and return to them after a few drinks of blood but before the light of dawn.

C.   In some of these tales vampires appear in the form of bats.

D.   Many films about frightening vampires have been made in recent years.

E.   In *Nosferatu*, the title character is a vampire with sharp teeth who resembles a rat.

1.   Many people died of consumption during the nineteenth century.

2.   Although its exact location is unknown, somewhere in the Dragoon Mountains lies the burial spot of Cochise, chief of the Chiricahua Apaches.

3.   They drove to the beach to have some fun in the sun.

4.   Bob had placed his lecture notes for his literature class in the file for his physics notes by mistake.

5.   Some viewers who spend too much time in front of their television sets can't distinguish the programs from real life.

21.6 CONJUNCTIONS

Directions: In each of the following sentences, first underline each conjunction. Then label each as a coordinating, subordinating, or correlative conjunction and explain its role in the sentence.

Example: <u>After</u> she had eaten the day-old pastry, Jill became ill.

Subordinating conjunction introduces adverb dependent clause that modifies verb "became": the clause answers the question "When (did Jill become ill)?"

A.   The United States Senate has sixteen standing committees, and the House of Representatives has twenty-two.

B.   Either Joan or her sister will attend tonight's concert.

C.   Inventors who receive a patent from the U.S. government may exclude all others from making, using, or selling the product of their imagination.

D.   Flamingos are pink because they eat so many shrimp.

E.   Slowly but surely, the hikers approached the top of the mountain.

1.   Jerry was late not only more often than Penny but also more often than anyone else in the class.

2.   Since he won the lottery, George's lifestyle has changed dramatically.

3.   Tom did not know where Rita had moved, nor did he care.

4.   We can't afford to take a trip to Paris unless we make our reservations months in advance.

5.   The new Hungarian wine that we ordered was tasty yet surprisingly inexpensive.

21.7   Review Exercise 1: Identifying Parts of Speech

Directions: Identify the part of speech of each italicized word in the following paragraph.

Yes, lawyers are *sometimes* criticized for defending criminals. *However,* their critics often overlook a crucial fact: people charged with crimes *are* not always guilty of *those* crimes. The U.S. legal *system*, which is based on *the* principle that those accused of breaking the law shall be regarded *as* innocent until proven guilty, *was designed* to protect innocent people *from* unjust treatment. By serving as advocates for the accused, attorneys *play* an important role in guaranteeing the rights of *those* brought to trial. One result, unfortunately, is that those *who* are guilty of crimes must also be treated as if they are *innocent until* they have been convicted in *a* court of law. Put simply, one justification for such a procedure is that it is *better* to let *some* criminals escape justice than to *unjustly* punish an innocent *person*.

21.8   REVIEW EXERCISE 2: IDENTIFYING PARTS OF SPEECH

Directions: Identify the part of speech of each italicized word in the following paragraph.

Venice, *one* of Europe's *most* famous cities, is *slowly* becoming flooded. The sea level *near* the city has risen more than four inches *during* the past *century*. Worse yet, the land upon which *it* is built has sunk at least eight inches. Experts predict that global *sea* levels will rise *another* eight inches *by* the year 2050. *If that* happens, the city's famed waterways *will inundate* the city for six months each year. *Have these* predictions *alarmed* the city leaders? *Yes!* In response, several plans to save Venice have *recently* been proposed *and* *more* are being formulated.

PART 6
SENTENCES

22.1 IDENTIFYING SIMPLE AND COMPLETE SUBJECTS

Directions: In the following sentences, underline the complete subject and write **SS** over the simple subject or subjects.

Example: <u>Many of the volunteers</u> were already experienced recyclers.

A. Scorpions, rattlesnakes, gila monsters, and black widow spiders inhabit the deserts of Arizona.

B. A day at the beach is always relaxing.

C. Sunken Spanish treasure ships laden with gold, silver, and gems are still being discovered in the Caribbean.

D. Bring me some dinner right now!

E. Moving to a new city can be stressful.

1. It might be late when you get home.

2. There were numerous large pelicans on the wharf yesterday.

3. My mother's collection of Wedgwood vases is on display in the lighted cabinet in the living room.

4. To climb Mt. Everest was always José's dream.

5. The student representatives and the college dean agreed to meet next Wednesday.

22.2   IDENTIFYING PREDICATES

Directions: In each of the following sentences, underline the complete subject once and the complete predicate twice. Then label the simple subject or subjects SS and the simple predicate or predicates P.

         SS   *SS P   P*

Example: <u>My mother and her first cousin</u> <u><u>are coming to our house for dinner tonight</u></u>.

A.   Where did you put the adding machine?

B.   At air shows stunt pilots put their planes into steep power stalls and then slip into dives.

C.   There is no film in a digital camera.

D.   In 1856, Gail Borden discovered a way to keep milk from spoiling and soon became rich.

E.   At last night's concert people were standing in the aisles, jumping up and down, and cheering wildly

    for the band to continue playing.

1.   The frequent shark attacks haven't done much for the island's tourist industry.

2.   When will the major airlines begin their holiday sales?

3.   The doctors and nurses on the night shift treated the burn victims from the four-alarm fire.

4.   Why have the FBI agents been questioning your neighbors?

5.   On the top of the cabinet were the missing photographs and the other documents.

22.3 IDENTIFYING COMPLEMENTS AND OTHER SENTENCE ELEMENTS—SET 1

Directions: Label any of these complements or elements that you find in the following sentences: **S** (subject), **AV** (active verb), **LV** (linking verb), **DO** (direct object), **IO** (indirect object), **OC** (object complement), **PA** (predicate adjective), **PN** (predicate nominative).

       S   LV PA

Example: The hotel guests were late for breakfast.

A.   Cemeteries in New Orleans contain many above-ground tombs.

B.   Marlene gave Tom her car keys yesterday.

C.   Similes and metaphors are common figures of speech.

D.   The Smiths are painting their new house purple.

E.   Drip irrigation is a very efficient method for watering a garden.

1.   People have marked birds in various ways since the times of the Roman Empire.

2.   However, scientific bird banding did not become common until the beginning of the twentieth century.

3.   The judges declared Fred the winner of the hundred-meter dash.

4.   The murder suspect appeared nervous and distracted at the preliminary hearing.

5.   Franklin Delano Roosevelt was the only American president elected to four terms.

22.4 IDENTIFYING COMPLEMENTS AND OTHER SENTENCE ELEMENTS—SET 2

Directions: Label any of these complements or sentence elements that are contained in the following sentences: **S** (subject), **AV** (active verb), **LV** (linking verb), **DO** (direct object), **IO** (indirect object), **OC** (object complement), **PA** (predicate adjective), **PN** (predicate nominative).

        S   *LV*   *PN*

Example: Seabiscuit was a famous racehorse in the 1930s.

A.   The statues found in the tombs of ancient Egypt have brought us many surprises.

B.   The Egyptians carved some of the statues from anorthosite gneiss.

C.   These appear deep blue in the sunlight.

D.   Other statues are huge and commemorate the power and accomplishments of the pharaohs.

E.   The Egyptians considered the tombs' life-sized statues, astonishingly realistic and beautifully painted, repositories of the *ka*, or soul, of the dead.

1.   Many royal tombs also contained dozens of small statues.

2.   These would be servants for the deceased in the afterlife.

3.   Priests brought these statues ritual foods and other offerings.

4.   A few tombs also contained finely sculpted heads.

5.   These heads may have been spares or may have been components in magical rites. *

* Adapted from Bennett Schiff, "Out of Egypt: Art in the Age of the Pyramids," *Smithsonian* 30.6 (1999): 108–119.

22.5 IDENTIFYING FRAGMENTS

Directions: Identify each of the following as either a complete sentence or a fragment by writing **S** or **F** on the blank.

Example:

We love to watch old movies. *S*

Because they are so entertaining. *F*

A. The first transatlantic cable linked America and Europe in 1886. _____

Which improved communication between the two continents immensely. _____

B. Being more independent and easier to maintain. _____

Has made cats rather than dogs Americans' favorite pet. _____

C. Since we had left the party early. _____

We made it home before the snowstorm. _____

D. Foods such as Greek bread, Chinese *jai*, and Italian roast chicken. _____

Holding religious significance for some people. _____

E. Having been appointed in 1922. _____

Rebecca Latimer Felton of Georgia was the first woman to serve in the United States

Senate. _____

1. When potatoes first appeared in Europe during the 1600s. _____

They were believed to cause venereal disease. _____

2. Since 1979, because of a proposal made by the United States. _____

The World Meteorological Association has given hurricanes male and female names. _____

3. Planning to be ready to leave. _____

Whenever you get here with your van. _____

4.   If you close your draperies and blinds to block out the sun's heat.   _____

     To keep your apartment cool during the day.   _____

5.   Avoid writing fragments.   _____

     It's not that hard to do.   _____

22.6 TYPES OF SENTENCES: IDENTIFYING INDEPENDENT AND DEPENDENT CLAUSES— SET 1

Directions: In each of the following sentences, underline each dependent clause once and each independent clause twice. Then, on the line below, identify the sentence type as simple, compound, complex, or compound-complex.

Example: <u>Everyone</u> <u>who has purchased a ticket</u> <u>will be admitted</u>.

complex

A. Some adventurous climbers use ice axes, spiked boots, and crampons to scale frozen waterfalls, but their success really depends on skill, stamina, and steady nerves.

_____

B. On October 12, 1999, the world's population reached six billion, according to the United Nations Fund for Population Activities.

_____

C. Hybrid bicycles, which can be very expensive, are a cross between mountain bicycles and racers; some cyclists refer to them as cross-terrain models.

_____

D. Because they had studied hard all semester, the students performed well on the physics exam.

_____

E. Moving south through Vermont, New Hampshire, Massachusetts, and Connecticut, the Connecticut River eventually reaches the Atlantic Ocean.

_____

1. Whereas an ophthalmologist is a medical doctor who specializes in treating the eyes, an optometrist is not a medical doctor; however, he or she is still qualified to examine eyes and write medical prescriptions.

_____

2. Ironically, wildlife conservation must sometimes include selective culling of endangered animals that
    are prospering.

    _____

3. Since most of the nations of the European Union adopted the euro as their currency, American
    currency has not been as strong in the European market.

    _____

4. We had a great time at the Salinas Rodeo last summer, so we will definitely go again next year.

    _____

5. If you go shopping at the flea market, you should inspect all items carefully and be prepared to
    haggle over prices.

    _____

22.7   TYPES OF SENTENCES: IDENTIFYING INDEPENDENT AND DEPENDENT CLAUSES— SET 2

Directions: In each of the following sentences, underline each dependent clause once and each independent clause twice. Then, on the line below, identify the sentence type as simple, compound, complex, or compound-complex.

Example: <u>Since she moved to a warmer climate,</u> <u>Lucille has become a friendlier person.</u>

   complex

A.   Poland's Wielicaka salt mine, which has been in use since the thirteenth century, contains many beautiful sculptures carved from the salt by generations of miners.

_____

B.   The search party has been looking all day for the missing hikers, but they seem to have vanished without leaving a trace.

_____

C.   Large amounts of fresh water pouring into the ocean from flooded rivers can hurt some kinds of sea life, especially shellfish.

_____

D.   Many people believe that King Arthur, the ruler of Camelot, was a real person, but no conclusive proof of his existence has ever been found.

_____

E.   Look under your chair if you are really brave.

_____

1.   In the Northeast the winters are harsh and cold; however, in the Southwest they are mild and warm.

_____

2.   Many well-known actors, such as Peter Coyote and Amy Madigan, narrate documentaries for PBS
      but do not appear on camera.

      _____

3.   Because the 9-11 terrorist attacks changed the nature of their business practices, U.S. shipping ports
      and chemical plants have increased security to ensure the safety of cargo, workers, and nearby
      residents.

      _____

4.   African termites, which dig as deep as 250 feet in search of water, sometimes bring particles of gold to
      the surface, so ancient African miners used to examine termite droppings to find deposits of gold.

      _____

5.   Nurseries that wholesale Christmas trees have discovered a way to increase their off-season income.

      _____

22.8   KINDS OF SENTENCES

Directions: Identify each of the following sentences by writing **declarative, interrogative,** or **exclamatory** in the blank after the sentence.

Example: Hey, get off my foot!

exclamatory

A.   Why would anyone want to vacation in Alaska in the winter?

_____

B.   Leap year occurs every four years.

_____

C.   Stop working on your exam and turn it in now.

_____

D.   No, I will do no such thing!

_____

E.   Joyce never understood why he enjoys those silly comedies.

_____

1.   Can we really believe the weather forecasts?

_____

2.   I should ask Willie what he wants for dinner.

_____

3.   Don't park on the left side of the street on street sweeping days.

_____

4.   Wow! What a surprise!

_____

5.   Have some of this delicious pumpkin pie.

_____

23.1   PREPOSITIONAL PHRASES

Directions: In each of the following sentences, enclose each prepositional phrase in parentheses and label the preposition **P** and the object(s) of the preposition **OP**. Then tell whether the prepositional phrase serves as an **adjective** or an **adverb**.

adverb   *adjective*
P   OP   P   OP

Example: The sailors returned home (at the end) (of the journey).

A.   The family of Mexican immigrants drove across the country in five days.

B.   In the middle of the night our fears seem much greater than they do during the daytime.

C.   The swarm of locusts appeared in our area during the early summer and really annoyed us with their noise.

D.   Wetlands provide ecological bases for wildlife; however, they are quite vulnerable to development, which has destroyed most of them in the continental United States.

E.   A crown of rubies, emeralds, and diamonds worn by many ancient British kings is now on display in the Tower of London's jewelry museum.

1.   There are many legends about vampires in many cultures throughout the world.

2.   Between 1986 and 1992, the percentage of all record sales represented by rock music fell from 47 percent to 36 percent.

3.   In an aquafarm lobsters can reach weights of one pound in a month; in the sea they need six months for that kind of growth.

4.   Put the sofa between the two bookshelves on the right side of the room.

5.   In 1993, a small hurricane struck the barrier islands off the coast of the Carolinas during the tourist season.

23.2   VERBAL PHRASES—SET 1

Directions: Underline the verbal phrase in each of the following sentences; identify it as a **gerund**, **participial**, or **infinitive phrase**; and explain its function in the sentence.

Example: I expect <u>to receive a large check</u> in the mail today.

infinitive phrase—acts as a noun; direct object of verb "expect"

A.   Many war-game enthusiasts re-create battles of the past by using miniature soldiers and carefully reconstructed battlefields.

B.   The scientists, concerned about the potential health hazards, made their most recent research findings public.

C.   Stretching for several blocks, the traffic jam tested the commuters' patience.

D.   To visit the Baseball Hall of Fame is the dream of many young boys.

E.   Swimming two or three times a week can keep a person in good health.

1.   To awaken every morning at 4:00 a.m., Levi Hutchins invented the alarm clock in 1787.

2.   Borrowing an idea from European law enforcement, some U.S. state police units are now using cameras at intersections.

3.   Kimba's motivation to finish her science project was impressive.

4.   Mary Lou found cooking the Thanksgiving turkey more work than she had originally anticipated.

5.   Trained for hunting small burrowing animals, the dachshund did not originate in Germany but instead came from Egypt.

23.3   VERBAL PHRASES—SET 2

Directions: In each of the following sentences, underline the verbal phrase; identify it as a **gerund,** **participial,** or **infinitive phrase**; and explain its function in the sentence.

Example: Mabel enjoys <u>eating sushi</u>.

gerund phrase—acts as noun; direct object of verb "enjoys"

A. Dying at a rate of about one species every 1,000 years, dinosaurs during the "great dying" actually took 50 to 75 million years to become extinct.

B. Jack's plan to find the buried treasure was really a futile daydream.

C. We were quite eager to reach our destination.

D. Finishing the last chapter of her novel was much more difficult than the author had anticipated.

E. Brazil, motivated by the need for an additional energy source, has produced gasohol from sugar as a viable alternative to gasoline.

1. Gertrude Ederle was the first woman to swim the English Channel.

2. Now spanning a short canal off the Colorado River, London Bridge is no longer falling down.

3. One of the major goals of psychology is learning how emotions influence behavior.

4. To honor Louis Sockalexis, the first Native American who played professional baseball, the Cleveland Naps changed their name to the Cleveland Indians in 1914.

5. Archaeologists working under strenuous conditions in the Arctic discovered dolls more than five hundred years old.

23.4   IDENTIFYING OTHER PHRASES AND THEIR FUNCTIONS

Directions: Identify the italicized phrase in each of the following sentences by writing **verb, prepositional, appositive,** or **absolute phrase** in the blank. Then explain its function in the sentence.

Example: John, *my oldest brother*, used to travel to Scandinavia every summer.

  appositive phrase—renames "John," the subject of the sentence

A.   *Many requests for assistance having been made,* the victims of Hurricane Katrina waited for help from FEMA.

_____

B.   The first subway was built in London *between 1860 and 1863.*

_____

C.   The Alamo, *an old Spanish mission in San Antonio,* was the site of a famous battle during the Texas War of Independence.

_____

D.   A devastating worldwide influenza epidemic killed many Americans *at the end of World War I.*

_____

E.   Some of the Pink Floyd fans *have been considering* camping out all night to be at the head of the ticket line tomorrow morning.

_____

1.   The native religion of Japan is called *Shinto*, *a word that means "the way of the Gods."* [Note: *Shinto* is italicized because it is a word used as a word, not because it is part of the italicized phrase to be identified.]

_____

2.   *All cargo having been locked in place,* the moving van left for its destination.

_____

3. We *will* definitely *be waiting* for you on the train platform.

   _____

4. Stephen King is one *of the most popular contemporary American writers.*

   _____

5. Celebration, Florida, *a town planned and built by the Disney Corporation,* has inspired at least two

   books.

   _____

24.1   IDENTIFYING INDEPENDENT AND DEPENDENT CLAUSES—SET 1

Directions: In each of the following sentences, underline any dependent clause once and any independent clause twice. Box any subordinating conjunctions. Then on the line below identify the dependent clause as **adverb, adjective,** or **noun** and explain its function in the sentence.

Example: ☐After☐ you have finished doing the laundry, you can wash the dishes.

adverb dependent clause—modifies verb "can wash"

A.   Ice cream, which was commercially made as early as 1786, was first sold in New York.

_____

B.   Whoever opens the door will be surprised by our Halloween costumes.

_____

C.   Anyone who decides to run for president must file a financial statement with the Federal Election

Commission.

_____

D.   Jacques Cousteau invented the aqualung while he was a member of the French Underground during

World War II.

_____

E.   Hawaii is the only one of the United States that produces coffee.

_____

1.   The ancient Romans thought that a crooked nose was a sign of leadership ability.

_____

2.   Unless you file a "Hold Mail" form, the post office will continue to deliver your mail while you are

away from home.

_____

3. The Ford Foundation, which was founded in 1936, has contributed funds to provide wheelchairs, jobs, and rehabilitation services for Vietnamese victims of Agent Orange.

    _____

4. The dog that lives next door dug up all the bulbs that we had planted last week.

    _____

5. Before they receive a black belt in tae kwon do, students must master nine forms, successfully spar with two opponents, and break two boards.

    _____

24.2   IDENTIFYING INDEPENDENT AND DEPENDENT CLAUSES—SET 2

Directions: In each of the following sentences, underline any dependent clause once and any independent clause twice. Box any subordinating conjunctions. Then on the line below identify each dependent clause as **adverb**, **adjective**, or **noun** and explain its function in the sentence.

Example: Before you turn in your exam, double-check your answers.

adverb dependent clause—modifies verb "double-check"

A.   While Samuel Johnson was compiling his famous dictionary, he employed the services of four

assistants.

_____

B.   How Nigel keeps that car running is a mystery to us.

_____

C.   Rasheed accepted an offer to play professional basketball in Poland although he would have preferred

to stay in the United States.

_____

D.   Mrs. Tyler advertised for a housekeeper who would shop for groceries, prepare meals, and do

laundry.

_____

E.   The Internet has profoundly changed the ways that stocks are bought and sold.

_____

1.   Although the porpoise is a graceful animal, its name is derived from two Latin words meaning "pig

fish."

_____

2.   What he says and what he does are sometimes two vastly different things.

_____

3.   When the actress arrived at the theatre, she was mobbed by reporters and photographers.

_____

4.   The player who wins this match will be eligible to compete in the finals.

_____

5.   We have never been as bored as we have been since moving to this small town.

_____

24.3 IDENTIFYING NOUN CLAUSES AND THEIR FUNCTIONS

Directions: In the following sentences, underline each noun dependent clause; then on the line below tell what role it plays in the sentence to complete the independent clause.

Example: <u>Whichever movie you choose</u> will be fine with me.

subject of sentence

A. Some people once believed that the world was flat.

_____

B. How Houdini performed many of his amazing feats remains a mystery to this day.

_____

C. Ted will give the jackpot to whoever shows up with the winning lottery ticket.

_____

D. We realized Harold's daughters only come to visit on alternate Fridays.

_____

E. Knowing what was expected of them enabled the gymnasts to perform their routines effortlessly.

_____

1. Angie will tell whoever is listening stories about her childhood.

_____

2. Jane said that her train would be late tonight.

_____

3. Whatever excuse Fred offers for missing the final exam probably won't convince his instructor.

_____

4. Mary doesn't know why you stopped speaking to her.

_____

5. We can travel to whatever Caribbean island seems warmest for our winter vacation.

_____

24.4   IDENTIFYING ADJECTIVE CLAUSES AND THEIR FUNCTIONS

Directions: In each of the following sentences, underline each adjective/relative clause and on the line below tell what word it modifies.

Example: That is the house <u>where I live</u>.

modifies "house"

A.   The city council's parking permit proposal, which was too long and needlessly complex, was

nevertheless adopted by a majority vote.

_____

B.   AmTrak has added three more trains that will travel directly between Boston and New York.

_____

C.   The interns who were hired last summer will be staying on full time.

_____

D.   The answers that you gave didn't make sense.

_____

E.   Horace, whom you had recommended for the job, did not impress the interviewer.

_____

1.   The neighbors expected the cat that was usually in their backyard to crawl into their van when they

moved away.

_____

2.   Students who study for each class do better on exams than those who cram the night before their

tests.

_____

3.   Angus cattle, which originated in Scotland, have become a very popular breed in America.

_____

4. The numbers that we use today, which are commonly called *Arabic numbers*, were actually invented by the people of India and are sometimes called *Hindu numbers*.

    _____

5. So that's the reason why no one lives on this street!

    _____

24.5   IDENTIFYING RESTRICTIVE AND NONRESTRICTIVE CLAUSES—SET 1

Directions: In the following sentences, underline each relative/adjective clause and identify it as **restrictive** or **nonrestrictive** by writing R or N-R in the blank. If it is nonrestrictive (not essential to the meaning of the sentence), enclose it in commas.

Example:

N-R   George's new pickup truck, <u>which is painted green</u>, is parked in the driveway.

A.   _____   Runners who stretch before they run have fewer injuries than those who don't stretch.

B.   _____   Nylon which can be woven into delicate lingerie can also be incorporated into durable machinery parts.

C.   _____   The potato is one of the major food crops that originated in America.

D.   _____   The lawyer whom I hired is a specialist in work accident litigation.

E.   _____   Air bags which were once considered impractical luxury features are now standard equipment on most vehicles.

1.   _____   Mary's swollen leg which she injured when she tripped on the jutting edge of the sidewalk may be tender for several weeks.

2.   _____   The baseball player who was from Mexico had been a celebrity in his country before moving to the United States.

3.   _____   The plants that need the most care should be placed in the well-lit window.

4.   _____   The picnickers whom the ants had annoyed moved three times before packing up and leaving the park.

5.   _____   My father who has worked all of his life will finally retire in September.

24.6 IDENTIFYING RESTRICTIVE AND NONRESTRICTIVE CLAUSES—SET 2

Directions: In the following sentences, underline each relative/adjective clause and identify it as **restrictive** or **nonrestrictive** by writing **R** or **N-R** in the blank. If it is nonrestrictive (not essential to the meaning of the sentence), enclose it in commas.

Example:

_____*R*_____ The doctor <u>whom you asked to see</u> is not taking any new patients right now.

A. _____ Robotic surgery which is still considered experimental has the highest success rate in the treatment of prostate cancer.

B. _____ The man who sat next to me on the subway picked my pocket.

C. _____ To understand the British system of nobility which is usually referred to as *the peerage* one needs to know something about British history.

D. _____ The proposal that got the most votes was not the one that we supported.

E. _____ The hours of the after-school day-care program are meant to accommodate children whose parents work evenings.

1. _____ Mauna Kea which is the highest peak in Hawaii is an extinct volcano.

2. _____ Martha's cousin Mabel who lived with her last summer is now attending nursing school.

3. _____ The pine-tree shilling was one of several coins that were minted in the American colonies before the Revolutionary War.

4. _____ John Donne who was born into a Catholic family was the dean of St. Paul's Cathedral and the most famous Anglican sermon writer of his day.

5. _____ The computer that Pete bought three years ago is already obsolete.

24.7   IDENTIFYING ADVERB CLAUSES AND THEIR FUNCTIONS

Directions: In each of the following sentences, underline each adverb clause and identify the word that it modifies—**verb, adjective,** or **adverb**—on the line below. Box any subordinating conjunctions.

Example: ☐After☐ heavy rain has fallen, one sometimes sees a rainbow.

modifies verb "sees"

A.   Artists have favored oil paint for hundreds of years because it dries slowly and does not crack.

_____

B.   After the hurricane the waves were larger than any we had ever seen before.

_____

C.   Bob and Karen were running as quickly as they could move to catch the train pulling out of the

station.

_____

D.   Although the word *hound* once referred to any kind of dog, it is now mainly used to indicate certain

types of hunting dogs.

_____

E.   When it's noon in Boston in the summer, it's 6 a.m. in Hawaii.

_____

1.   The final exam questions were harder than I had expected them to be.

_____

2.   Even though computers today have reached an amazing level of speed and sophistication, future

computer chips may perform 250 million calculations per second.

_____

3.   After he discovered the relationship between bacteria and infection, Joseph Lister revolutionized
      medicine by developing antiseptic surgical procedures.

      _____

4.   This computer's programs load more slowly than the ones in the new model do.

      _____

5.   Ned told his prom date that she looked lovelier than she had ever looked before.

      _____

25.1   SUBJECT–VERB AGREEMENT: PERSON AND NUMBER, DELAYED SUBJECTS

Directions: In each of the following sentences, underline the simple subject or subjects and box the correct verb form contained in the parentheses.

Example: There (is , are) plenty of soup for everyone.

A.   One of the sofas (need, needs) to be dusted.

B.   The coach as well as the captains (lead, leads) the pep rallies.

C.   On the horizon (lie, lies) the tip of the volcano.

D.   Where (is, are) the box of explosives?

E.   The singer, along with the rest of the band, (is, are) being interviewed on the radio show.

1.   Here (is, are) my recipe for dumplings.

2.   (Do, Does) the pitcher and catcher make up new signs for every inning?

3.   At the start of the movie, from under the turbulent waves (emerge, emerges) a huge whale.

4.   Another batch of cookies (is, are) ready to be taken out of the oven.

5.   Why (was, were) that pile of photographs left on the floor?

25.2 SUBJECT–VERB AGREEMENT: COMPOUND SUBJECTS, COLLECTIVE NOUNS

Directions: In each of the following sentences, underline the simple subject or subjects and box the correct verb form contained in the parentheses.

Example: The city <u>council</u> (is, ⎡are⎤) voting on the measure today.

A.   Neither the buyers nor the seller (know, knows) about all of the house's defects.

B.   My art history teacher and adviser (is, are) an expert on Renaissance painting.

C.   The news about the earthquakes in Pakistan (was, were) terrifying.

D.   Pork and beans (is, are) the only meal that Ralph can cook.

E.   The faculty (is, are) concerned about their new offices.

1.   Both the captain and the first mate (was, were) responsible for the accident.

2.   Either Harold or his sisters (is, are) going to the fireworks display with us tonight.

3.   The jury (was, were) sequestered for three days before reaching a verdict.

4.   Marlene declared that strawberries and cream (was, were) her favorite dessert.

5.   The football team (is, are) scheduled to play in Dallas next week.

25.3   SUBJECT–VERB AGREEMENT: NUMBERS AND NUMERICAL TERMS AS SUBJECTS

Directions: In each of the following sentences, underline the subject or subjects and box the correct verb form contained in the parentheses.

Example: <u>Ten dollars</u> (is , are) too much to pay for a movie ticket.

A.   A percentage of the profits (was, were) given to charity each year.

B.   The number of applicants for the job (is, are) increasing by the hour.

C.   Twenty bushes of poison ivy (was, were) cut along the pathway.

D.   A number of mountains in Colorado (is, are) more than 14,000 feet tall.

E.   Six hours (was, were) too much time to spend filling out the accident report.

1.   One-third of the students (has, have) taken this course before.

2.   A number of protesters, police, and innocent bystanders (was, were) injured during the

demonstrations.

3.   Three-quarters of the pie (has, have) already been eaten.

4.   Fifteen years of commuting on that freeway (was, were) more than I could take.

5.   The number of oil spills on the Pacific Coast (has, have) doubled during the previous decade.

25.4 SUBJECT–VERB AGREEMENT: RELATIVE AND INDEFINITE PRONOUNS AS SUBJECTS

Directions: In each of the following sentences, underline the simple subject or subjects and box the correct verb form contained in the parentheses.

Example: <u>Each</u> of the contestants ($\boxed{\text{is}}$, are) required to attend tonight's event.

A.   Nobody except the night watchman (has, have) a key to the safe.

B.   Most of the snow (has, have) already fallen.

C.   Everything in the files (has, have) been carefully scrutinized.

D.   Avian flu is one of the viruses that (has, have) the potential to become a dangerous pandemic.

E.   Some of the trees in the yard (has, have) Dutch Elm disease.

1.   Another of the suspects (has, have) confessed to the crime.

2.   Everyone in the bleachers (was, were) cheering wildly as the runner crossed the finish line.

3.   Most of the students (has, have) taken the prerequisite for this course.

4.   Mohammad is the only one of the contestants who (know, knows) the answer.

5.   Neither of the dinner guests (is, are) waiting in the hall.

25.5   OTHER SUBJECT–PREDICATE ERRORS

Directions: In each of the following sentences, underline the simple subject or subjects and box the correct verb form contained in the parentheses.

Example: The Oriental <u>vases</u> ($\boxed{\text{was}}$, were) the prize given to the winner.

A.   Tonight's dinner special (is, are) spaghetti and meatballs.

B.   *The Martian Chronicles* (is, are) a complex book.

C.   His consuming interest (was, were) old stamps and coins.

D.   *Organic ingredients* (is, are) a misleading phrase on the labels of products whose content is not at least

       95 percent organic.

E.   These primitive paintings (is, are) considered the artist's best work.

1.   During its first season, *Desperate Housewives* (was, were) the most watched new television series.

2.   Quilts and other traditional handicrafts (is, are) now known as *folk art.*

3.   *Consenting adults* (is, are) a term that means different things to different people.

4.   Marcia's grades (is, are) the only thing that matters to her parents.

5.   *Rivers of Steel* (was, were) printed in big bold letters on the cover of the novel.

25.6 PRONOUN–ANTECEDENT AGREEMENT—SET 1

Directions: In each of the following sentences, underline the antecedent or antecedents of the pronoun and box the correct pronoun form contained in the parentheses.

Example: The oil <u>company</u> raised (its, |their|) prices after the embargo had been announced.

A.   Neither the children nor Mrs. Greene could find (her, their) directions to the theatre.

B.   Everything, including the tools, was in (its, their) proper place on the shelf.

C.   The horse (who, that) escaped was an expensive thoroughbred.

D.   No one was able to finish (his, his or her, their) exam in the allotted time.

E.   The crew gathered on deck to discuss (its, their) strategy for the big race.

1.   The supervisor asked each of the workers to submit (his or her, their) vacation requests by Friday.

2.   Either my father or your uncle will join us on the camping trip, so (he, they) will need to bring camping gear.

3.   Anyone who thinks that (he, he or she, they) can cheat on this exam should think again.

4.   All students must know (his or her, their) university identification numbers.

5.   A firefighter must be prepared to risk (his, his or her, their) life to rescue people.

25.7   PRONOUN–ANTECEDENT AGREEMENT—SET 2

Directions: In each of the following sentences, box the incorrect pronoun form or forms and write the correct form(s) in the blank. If the sentence is correct, write **OK** in the blank.

Example: The family is planning ⬚their⬚ summer vacation.

its

A.   Many researchers are now studying the causes of heart failure to prevent it.

_____

B.   Before an architect designs a house, he must first understand his clients' lifestyle.

_____

C.   The dog who barked all night lives next door.

_____

D.   Everyone on the boys' soccer team is responsible for keeping his equipment in working order.

_____

E.   Every member of the group expressed their dismay at the outcome of the election.

_____

1.   Neither Tommy nor Percy can understand their math homework.

_____

2.   He is the kind of patient which dentists hate to treat.

_____

3.   The committee submitted their revised budget last week.

_____

4.   Neither of the daughters remembered their mother's birthday.

_____

5.   Someone forgot their laptop computer in the library.

_____

25.8   AMBIGUOUS AND VAGUE ANTECEDENTS

Directions: Revise each of the following sentences to correct the problem caused by an ambiguous or vague antecedent.

Example:

Original sentence: Insurance rates continue to climb; this is why some people choose not to own a car.

Possible revision: Insurance rates continue to climb; some people choose not to own a car because of these increases.

A.   Jack went to visit David after he returned from his vacation.

B.   Brad is a senior citizen, which qualifies him for a discount at the movies.

C.   After my flight had been canceled and I had missed my connection, they put me up in a hotel and gave me vouchers for cabs and meals.

D.   Kevin plays his stereo full blast all night long, and his neighbors don't like it.

E.   Andrea left part of her car sticking out of the driveway, which caused it to be hit by a speeding truck.

1.   In today's newspaper it says that children today spend more time watching TV than their parents did.

2.   I contacted my bank after receiving a notice about a bounced check, but they didn't believe my explanation.

3.   The novels of Nadine Gorimer and André Brink explore the consequences of apartheid in the country where they were raised: South Africa.

4.   Catherine told Mary that she had been accepted for admission to the University of Pennsylvania.

5.   Several mysterious fires have occurred at the munitions factories; they should be investigated.

26.1 CORRECTING SENTENCE FRAGMENTS

Directions: In each numbered segment below, first underline each fragment. Then correct the fragment by making it part of the sentence in the segment.

Example:

The surfers kept heading out into the tall waves.
<u>Even though it was nearly dark.</u>

Possible revision: The surfers kept heading out into the tall waves even though it was nearly dark.

A.   The island of Britain actually contains three different countries.

Those being England, Scotland, and Wales.

B.   In some cultures it is a constant struggle for a woman to gain the respect of men.

Such as those that consider men more important than women.

C.   We were finally admitted to the exclusive nightclub.

After we tipped the doorman generously.

D.   Still visible after centuries of use and neglect.

Roman roads can be traced in many parts of Europe today.

E.   Unlike most rivers in North America, the Shenandoah flows north.

And empties into the Potomac.

1.   The state of Alaska has more than 100,000 glaciers.

Most of which are only visible from the air.

2.   Ginger has studied ballet and modern dance.

Since she was a child.

3.   Hours before the guests began arriving.

The servants had set the banquet table with the silver service.

4.   Ethiopian marathoners won seven Olympic gold medals.

      The first in 1960 and the last in 2000.

5.   Although light usually travels at about 186,000 miles per second.

      Scientists have slowed it down to 38 miles per hour.

26.2   CORRECTING COMMA SPLICES

Directions: In each of the following sentences, correct the comma splice by using one of the six methods discussed in Chapter 26. Be sure that all punctuation is used correctly.

Example:

Comma splice: Some people love to celebrate their birthdays, others try to forget about them.

Possible revision: Some people love to celebrate their birthdays, **but** others try to forget about them.

A.   Jack Kerouac used long, continuous rolls of paper while writing on his typewriter, he didn't like to waste time sticking in a new sheet.

B.   Some people talk on their cell phones while driving, they are a hazard to other drivers.

C.   Some comets orbit the earth every few years, other comets take thousands of years to circle the planet.

D.   Terry felt lucky yesterday, he bought a lottery ticket.

E.   Medical science has extended life expectancy, consequently people need to develop hobbies that can become meaningful activities in retirement.

1.   Cowrie shells are often found in tourist shops at beach resorts, they were once used as money in many parts of the world.

2.   Paula loves to travel, she's been to China, Russia, and Scandinavia in the past four years.

3.   On 1854, Commodore Matthew Perry persuaded the Japanese to open their borders, their country had been closed to foreigners for centuries.

4.   The English Channel Tunnel was designed to handle both rail and highway traffic, it has been nicknamed the "Chunnel."

5.   Many people consider popcorn a typical American food, it was also a favorite food in ancient times.

26.3 CORRECTING FUSED/RUN-ON SENTENCES

Directions: In each of the following items, correct the fused/run-on sentence by using one of the five methods discussed in Chapter 26. Add any transition words or punctuation that is needed.

Example:

Run-on: The *USS Constitution* was launched in 1797 it was nicknamed "Old Ironsides."

Possible revision: The *USS Constitution*, nicknamed "Old Ironsides," was launched in 1797.

A. Julia rarely got to play during soccer practice she didn't expect to score a goal in the game.

B. Some tides change approximately every twelve hours the moon is the cause of these massive shifts of ocean water.

C. Many people enjoy the freedom that comes with working at home they must be disciplined in order to be productive.

D. I arrived on campus at 8 a.m. this morning I still couldn't find a parking space.

E. High-frequency sound waves have many medical applications one is to determine the health and even the gender of a fetus in the womb.

1. Most home-video viewers have switched from VCRs to DVD players they are also watching films in theatres less often.

2. Drivers should always be aware of weather conditions for example, fog reduces visibility, and icy roads require very slow travel.

3. The Appalachian Trail is popular with hikers it runs from Georgia to Maine.

4. The Presidential Medal of Freedom is the highest civilian award given by the United States it was established in 1963 by President John F. Kennedy.

5. Many farmers have discovered that sunflowers are a very profitable crop they can sell the seeds for bird feed.

26.4 REVIEW EXERCISE: CORRECTING FRAGMENTS, COMMA SPLICES, AND RUN-ONS

Directions: Revise each of the following two paragraphs to eliminate sentence fragments, comma splices, and run-ons. As you revise, be sure to change capitalization, add conjunctions, and correct punctuation as needed.

A.

Although turquoise was mined by Egyptian pharaohs more than five thousand years ago. And traded by Chinese emperors for centuries. Most Americans associate this beautiful stone with their own desert southwest. For good reason. More than a thousand years ago, ancient Mayans were importing turquoise from what is now New Mexico. The mines were surprisingly large, archaeologists estimate that Native American miners dug thousands of tons of rock. Fewer than twenty active mines are in this country today, however, most of the turquoise dug now comes from China.

Adapted from Joseph Harris, "Tantalizing Turquoise,"
Smithsonian 30.5 (1999): 70–80.

1.

The original model for Dracula was Vlad the Impaler. A fifteenth-century warrior prince of Walachia in eastern Europe. According to Romanian legend, the sadistic Prince Vlad took his meals amid a forest of impaled, groaning victims, after each course Vlad washed down his food with his victim's blood. In the belief that it imbued him with supernatural strength. Vlad's crimes were legend imprisoned himself, he tortured mice and birds for amusement. His mountaintop retreat, known as Castle Drakula. Suggested the name of the vampire villain of novel and film fame.

Adapted from Charles Panati, *Extraordinary Origins of Everyday Things* (New York: Harper, 1987), 179–180.

26.5   SHIFTS IN SENTENCE CONSTRUCTION—SET 1

Directions: Revise each of the following sentences by correcting any shifts in person, tense, mood, or voice or any other mixed sentence pattern.

Example:

Original sentence: After Rosalie buys a python, she realized that it was a very dangerous pet.

Possible revision: After Rosalie had bought a python, she realized that it was a very dangerous pet.

A.   The Connecticut River, the longest waterway in New England, has drained an area of eleven thousand square miles as it flows from the Canadian border to Long Island Sound.

B.   First, an application form needs to be filled out by job candidates, and then ask for an interview.

C.   The psychology professor told Felix to hand in his paper by 2 p.m. and did he realize that its being three days late would affect his grade.

D.   Anyone planning on climbing Mt. Rainier needs to anticipate all of the hazards that they might encounter.

E.   Marcus said come on over for dinner and that we should bring some dessert.

1.   Mad cow disease occurs when uninfected cattle eat meat that contains infectious proteins and causes normal proteins in the brain to unfold.

2.   The emergency room nurse suggested that we be calm and did not let the patient sense our anxiety.

3.   One may catch the flu if you are often in crowded rooms in the winter.

4.   John mailed in the correct forms for the rebate but was never received.

5.   By writing this essay shows my true feelings about living in Arizona.

26.6   SHIFTS IN SENTENCE CONSTRUCTION—SET 2

Directions: Revise each of the following sentences by correcting any shifts in person, number, tense, mood, or voice or any other mixed sentence pattern.

Example:

Original sentence: Before you begin cleaning the computer's disk drive, one should close all other programs.

Possible revision: Before you begin cleaning the computer's disk drive, you should close all other programs.

A.   The proposal that was put forth to tear down city hall was made by the city council, not the mayor.

B.   Our desire to climb the last thousand feet of Mauna Kea volcano made us dizzy and lightheaded.

C.   A person should always look in all directions before they enter a crosswalk.

D.   The landlord said to put the key under the mat after viewing the apartment and that we shouldn't disturb the tenants in the building.

E.   When people sometimes twist facts about themselves, such as the places where they have worked, helps them save face.

1.   If one reviews the homework every day, you can learn a foreign language.

2.   Dreams are not necessarily accidental, for they were often considered efforts of the subconscious to work out real problems.

3.   We thought a light at the end of the tunnel is a sign of hope, but it was just on a train coming in our direction.

4.   Be on time for your interview, and you should always thank your interviewer at the end of the conference.

5.   The cheetah is very tired after chasing its quarry and usually rested for several minutes before eating.

26.7   FAULTY PARALLELISM

Directions: Edit each of the following sentences to correct the faulty parallelism.

Example:

Original sentence: Bob liked watching football on Sunday afternoons and to work on his car.

Possible revision: Bob liked watching football on Sunday afternoons and working on his car.

A.   Dragonflies can fly twenty-five miles per hour, take off backwards, and they have a 360-degree field of vision.

B.   Louise was surprised and in an excited state upon learning that she had won the dance competition.

C.   The superstitious English of the sixteenth and seventeenth centuries were afraid of moonless nights, and black cats terrified them.

D.   Working on the assembly line was not only physically exhausting, but it was also easy to get confused.

E.   The collapse of her business venture left Rose penniless, ill, and an angry woman.

1.   Good economists measure not only the confidence of consumers but also what percentage of the workforce is employed.

2.   To talk about helping the homeless is not the same as working in a soup kitchen.

3.   Guests at the inn enjoyed fine dining, great scenery, and the weather was mild.

4.   The airline clerk told us that the luggage was too heavy and that we would have to pay an extra charge.

5.   Microwaved foods have become very popular because of ease of preparation, they cook quickly, and are often very delicious.

26.8   MISPLACED AND DANGLING MODIFIERS—SET 1

Directions: Rewrite each of the following sentences to correct any misplaced or dangling modifiers. If a sentence is correctly written, write "Correct."

Example:

Original sentence: Running poorly and rusting quickly, I decided to repair my old car.

Possible revision: I decided to repair my old car because it was running poorly and rusting quickly.

A.   Nestled between two mountains, visitors can journey back to a town that has remained unchanged

 for two centuries.

B.   Many political candidates promise openly to deal with controversial issues.

C.   To play tennis well, frequent practice is needed.

D.   Arriving home after midnight, the house was dark.

E.   Since breaking my leg, Kent has helped me with my household chores.

1.   The hikers waded through the stream climbing to the summit.

2.   Marie served elegant watercress sandwiches to the ladies on her fine china.

3.   Unlike black bears, campers must remember that grizzlies can be very aggressive.

4.   Driving home in a daze, the police officer stopped me for running a red light.

5.   The picnic table and benches are on the lawn that we just finished painting.

26.9   MISPLACED AND DANGLING MODIFIERS—SET 2

Directions: Edit the following sentences to correct any misplaced or dangling modifiers. If a sentence is correctly written, write "Correct."

Example:

Original sentence: Before leaving for your vacation, the plants should be watered.

Possible revision: Before leaving for your vacation, you should water the plants.

A.   Waiting for the elevator to come, a mouse ran through the crowd.

B.   Wrapped, labeled, and addressed, the gifts were ready to be mailed.

C.   Martina heard that the rapist had been arrested on the ten o'clock news.

D.   The air traffic controller who worked cautiously guided Flight 774 to a safe landing.

E.   While visiting friends, my motorcycle was stolen.

1.   Dancing on their hind legs, the audience rose and started to cheer as the elephants entered the ring.

2.   Before submitting the project for a grade, the instructor insisted that we check our work carefully.

3.   Looking through old family photo albums, I found one of my mother's baby pictures.

4.   Eager to see Fort Sumter, the ferry took the tourists across Charleston Harbor.

5.   The archaeologists almost found a complete dinosaur skeleton.

26.10 AMBIGUOUS WORDING

Directions: Edit each of the following sentences to correct any incomplete comparisons or confusing logic.

Example: I have owned a parakeet longer than my brother | *has.*
                                                              ∧

A.   Tina has always but might not continue to subscribe to *Vogue.*

B.   Denver is larger than any city in Colorado.

C.   Manuel enjoys his sports car more than Linda.

D.   The hothouse tomatoes from the farm stand are as expensive but tastier than those from the gourmet market.

E.   Sri Lanka, formerly Ceylon, has and continues to be the world's chief supplier of natural cinnamon.

1.   Jane's answers to the quiz questions were better than the other contestants.

2.   Jake has and will continue to feel feverish and dizzy from his severe sunburn.

3.   My grandmother is older than any residents in her senior citizens' complex.

4.   The new investigative reporter was as good if not better than some of her more experienced co-workers.

5.   Cecilia's fish has more fins than her boyfriend.

26.11 NONSTANDARD LANGUAGE

Directions: Edit the following sentences to correct any nonstandard language.

Example:

Original sentence: The coach tried to get us psyched for the big game.

Possible revision: The coach tried to get us excited about the big game.

A.   You should of let us know that you would be arriving late.

B.   Gillian couldn't scarcely believe her luck when she found out that she'd won the big prize.

C.   The deejay played my favorite song from off the new Rolling Stones album.

D.   That child she was left unattended at the grocery store.

E.   Dorothy said that my outfit is so last year.

1.   The mechanic said that he was fixing to begin work on my car tomorrow.

2.   Your dad would not of known that you were out past curfew if you hadn't made so much noise when
     you got home.

3.   I can't hardly lift that big package.

4.   That shade of green looks kind a nice on you.

5.   We found it plenty easy to earn extra income by collecting returnables.

PART 7
PUNCTUATION AND MECHANICS

27.1 USING PERIODS

Directions: In each of the following sentences, correct any errors in the use of periods or other end-of-sentence punctuation. If there are no errors in a sentence, write "Correct."

Example: My cousins live in Fayetteville, ~~A. K.~~ *AK.*

A. Call me in the morning if you don't feel better!

B. Most states observe daylight-saving time (DST) (Arizona is the only state that doesn't.), but some counties within those states do not observe the seasonal time change.

C. Meet me at 10 am at the town clock.

D. The speaker was a former officer of the NAACP.

E. It took Phillip ten years to complete his Ph.D..

1. Park in the green zone (the red zone is only for faculty.) or you will get a ticket.

2. John asked if we should bring our own sleeping bags on the camping trip?

3. Zelda's aunt is an F.B.I. agent.

4. We were all proud of Aunt Helen, who received her B.A. in fine arts at the age of sixty-three.

5. Please respond with your information A.S.A.P.

27.2 USING QUESTION MARKS

Directions: In each of the following sentences, correct any errors in the use or omission of question marks. If a sentence is correct, write "Correct."

Scotland.
Example: He asked when you would return to ~~Scotland?~~

A.   Will you—can you?—repair my car before the end of the week?

B.   Am I supposed to know the answers to those difficult math problems??

C.   Really, why didn't I think of that.

D.   Mrs. Brown (is that her real name) claims to be a descendent of Napoleon.

E.   Would you please return these library books today?

1.   I wondered why he kept telling the same story?

2.   "Are you crazy," Leo asked? when he saw us walk out on the ice.

3.   Will you be visiting your aunt in North Dakota this year?

4.   You must catch the 7:13 a.m. train (do you have a choice) because it's the only one that stops in Mansfield.

5.   The doctor asked whether there were any volunteers for the experiment?

27.3 USING EXCLAMATION POINTS

Directions: In each of the following sentences, correct any errors in the use or omission of exclamation points. If a sentence contains no errors, write "Correct."

Example: Wow!*/* What a ridiculous answer*/*!

A.   "The car is rolling down the hill," Joe screamed!

B.   "I wish you would arrive on time," thundered Harold.

C.   "Hey!" Maureen yelled. "What are you doing in our basement?"

D.   Halt!! Who goes there?

E.   "Don't track that mud on my clean rug, or you'll be sorry?" exclaimed Aunt Tillie.

1.   What! You're not going to your sister's wedding!?

2.   Well, I guess I will attend after all!

3.   Here comes the tornado. Run for your life.

4.   Stop that thief!!

5.   Ouch! That really hurt!

28.1   USING COMMAS WITH COMPOUNDS AND IN COMPOUND SENTENCES

Directions: In each of the following sentences, correct any errors in comma use with compounds or in compound sentences. If a sentence is punctuated correctly, write "Correct."

Example: It rained heavily on Monday/ and snowed on Tuesday.

A.   Before going to the Philippines, we tried to teach ourselves Tagalog but we finally had to admit

defeat, and find a teacher to help us.

B.   We wanted to eat at the new Thai restaurant but, it was closed for repairs.

C.   People who have purchased advance tickets, and people who are Gold Card members may board the

airplane first.

D.   I had the flu last week so I had to miss the New Year's Eve party.

E.   Don't place anything flammable on the space heater, or near the halogen lamp.

1.   Jeannette Rankin was the first woman elected to the U.S. Congress, and the only member of the

House to vote against World War II.

2.   Isabel didn't want to hurt Pedro's feelings yet, she didn't really want to go on a date with him.

3.   The secretary forgot to mail my paycheck and my schedule of courses.

4.   Many patients now receive organ transplants but doctors still don't know how long these transplants

will continue to function.

5.   About one-third of the passengers on the *Mayflower* left England for religious reasons and, the other

two-thirds were adventurers.

28.2 USING COMMAS IN A SERIES

Directions: In each of the following sentences, correct any errors in the use or omission of commas with items in a series. If a sentence is correctly punctuated, write "Correct."

groups, and

Example: The charity solicits donations from businesses, civic ~~groups and,~~ individuals.

A. The Pleiades, Taurus, and Orion are three of the best-known winter constellations in the Northern Hemisphere.

B. Some colds begin with a runny nose, others begin with chills and still others, begin when a person feels excessively weak and tired.

C. A number of political parties, including, the Federalist Party, the Whig Party and the Democrat-Republican Party, played important roles in America's past.

D. Neither rain, nor sleet, nor snow delays the delivery of the U.S. mail.

E. Many pioneers brought little more than a rifle, an ax, a plowshare, and a few simple carpentry tools, on their journey west.

1. Office desks often come equipped with space for computers modems and fax machines.

2. Fred hated crowds, didn't like dealing with store clerks and could never find products he liked at the mall.

3. In the nineteenth century phrenologists believed that they could identify character traits such as, caution, kindness and, conscientiousness by examining the shape of a person's skull.

4. The captain, the flight attendants and the federal marshals were all aboard the plane.

5. "We have sealed all the hatches taken in all the sails and radioed for help," wrote the desperate sea captain.

28.3 USING COMMAS WITH MODIFIERS

Directions: In each of the following sentences, correct any errors in the use or omission of commas with modifiers. If a sentence is correctly punctuated, write "Correct."

Example: The artist took a slow **,** careful look at her finished canvas.

A. The moldy, dank smell in the cellar was caused by the porous walls that leaked whenever it rained.

B. Living near the ocean involves putting up with ever-present, long-legged, spiders and great numbers of tiny ants.

C. Modern farmers use systemic, cotton defoliants to allow mechanical harvesters easier access to opened bolls.

D. We picked a particularly, cold day to view the ice sculptures in the park.

E. Radio talk shows attract many outspoken opinionated callers.

1. More Americans are becoming familiar with the sharp piercing cry of the coyote.

2. The band played an unusually, long set at last night's concert.

3. Builders use strong lightweight plywood in almost every kind of construction project.

4. The small, hardy Lapps speak a language related to Finnish.

5. Sarah was an unusual, biology student who always examined each specimen with a curious penetrating eye.

28.4 USING COMMAS WITH INTRODUCTORY WORDS

Directions: In each of the following sentences, correct any errors in the use or omission of commas with introductory words. If a sentence is punctuated correctly, write "Correct."

street.

Example: Walking quickly across the ~~street~~ Mildred narrowly avoided being hit by the speeding car.

A.   To learn how to operate the new computer program you will need to study the manual.

B.   Wearing a beaded collar the poodle pranced around the ring.

C.   Built in 1769 and used to pull French artillery the world's first automobile, a steam carriage, was invented by Captain Nicolas Cugnot.

D.   Nevertheless we decided to leave the party early because we were tired.

E.   Soon after the laser was created in 1960 scientists began searching for ways to use it in medicine.

1.   Almost twice the size of the United States Siberia contains only one-sixth as many people.

2.   Until you remember, your secret code you won't be admitted through the security gate.

3.   Unlike the national security adviser the senator believed that the president needed a full accounting of events.

4.   On the other hand no one else agreed with him.

5.   Running in the marathon, had always been her dream.

28.5   USING COMMAS WITH ENDING WORDS

Directions: In each of the following sentences, insert or delete commas used with ending words to punctuate the sentence correctly. If a sentence is punctuated correctly, write "Correct."

Example: The winter solstice is celebrated on December 21 **,** which is the shortest day of the year.

A.   Mrs. Robinson's job involved entering data, that had been submitted by FBI agents from around the country.

B.   The intramural and intercollegiate teams will drop athletes who are convicted of substance abuse.

C.   The State Department's decoding unit hired the translator, who had lived in Iraq for seven years.

D.   The class enjoyed reading this version of the *Aeneid* which was written in the original Latin.

E.   We were surprised by the early arrival of Uncle Charles who always shows up extremely late for family gatherings.

1.   We bought tickets for the last night of the play's performance which is usually the least crowded.

2.   The graduating class honored the priest, whose center for the homeless has become a national model.

3.   Raoul bought the car, that had been given the highest rating in *Consumer Reports*.

4.   The ballplayers voted for the umpires, who they felt called the fairest game.

5.   They moved from a cold place, Bangor, Maine, to Detroit Lakes, Minnesota a place with even colder winters.

28.6   USING COMMAS WITH INTERRUPTING WORDS

Directions: In each of the following sentences, add or delete commas around interrupting words to punctuate the sentence correctly. If a sentence is punctuated correctly, write "Correct."

Example: My oldest brother , Fred, is now a senior at the University of Colorado.

A.   Bald eagles which can be found mainly in wilderness areas usually prefer a diet of fish.

B.   Frank's wife Darlene always knew all the neighborhood gossip first.

C.   The senior partner, who was the only one who understood the divorce laws, took my case.

D.   The Parthenon which was completed in 432 B.C. is the best surviving example of classical Greek architecture.

E.   The grant, that Fernando received, will provide him with a modest stipend so that he can finish his research.

1.   Katherine Anne Porter's only novel *Ship of Fools* was awarded the Pulitzer Prize.

2.   One of the violinists, who plays in the pops orchestra, will be selected to join the symphony orchestra at the end of the season.

3.   The instructor accepted Hilda's late term paper. She did however give it one grade lower than she would have if it had been submitted on time.

4.   Professional counseling in elementary school which is a relatively new phenomenon can make a dramatic difference in the scholastic performance of young children.

5.   Bram Stoker's famous novel, *Dracula,* has been made into several films as well as a Broadway musical.

28.7 USING COMMAS WITH DIALOGUE, INTERJECTIONS, AND TAGS

Directions: Edit the following sentences so that commas are used correctly with dialogue, interjections, and tags.

Jennifer,
Example: ~~Jennifer~~ have you seen my shawl?

A.   You my students are the first people to read my new story.

B.   Patrick Henry said "Give me liberty or give me death."

C.   "Why?" asked the hairdresser, "did you dye your hair pink?"

D.   The parking lot attendant said, that this lot is usually full by 10 a.m.

E.   "Let's leave Ellen," Brad said to his friend as he opened the door.

1.   "I'm so glad that you came to visit me" Aunt Mabel told her nephews "and I hope that you will stay

     for a few days."

2.   "Don't cross the street at that dangerous intersection you idiot!" yelled the crossing guard.

3.   "Why did you mail your Christmas packages so late?," asked her mother.

4.   "Well give me the car keys right now!" demanded Joe.

5.   There is another fire exit isn't there?

28.8   USING COMMAS WITH TITLES, INITIALS, ADDRESSES, AND NUMBERS

Directions: Edit the following sentences for correct comma use by adding or omitting commas with titles, initials, addresses, or numbers.

Arizona,
Example: Sedona, ~~Arizona~~ is at the entrance to Oak Creek Canyon.

A.   That quotation can be found on page 1,235.

B.   Jamie will begin his new job in November, 2007.

C.   America entered World War II on December 7, 1941 when Japanese planes attacked Pearl Harbor.

D.   The commencement speakers were Carolyn Williams Ph.D., and Robert Wilson, Jr., a local

philanthropist.

E.   The MacKay family has lived in Arlington, Virginia for many years but also has roots in York, Maine

and Edina, Illinois.

1.   Margaret Smith M.D. has opened a new office on Broadway.

2.   On September, 25 1890 the nation's second-oldest national park, Sequoia National Park, was

established.

3.   His college acceptance letter was dated 5 May, 2006.

4.   Martin received a check for $283,315 on Thursday July 15.

5.   Peter's mailing address is 59315 West Euclid Drive, Apartment 205, Phoenix, AZ, 85044.

28.9   USING COMMAS TO PREVENT CONFUSION

Directions: In each of the following sentences, add any commas that are necessary to prevent misreading or confusion.

long,

Example: Before ~~long~~ paths were easier to find in the woods.

A.   After all the packages did finally arrive.

B.   The mayor wanted answers not excuses from the commission.

C.   Before eating Ralph introduced all of the guests to each other.

D.   Those who serve serve us well.

E.   After losing the team didn't feel much like celebrating.

1.   He invested in the stock market hoping to make money not lose it.

2.   We had to return to the old house three times rather than once more often than we had expected to

      retrieve all of our possessions.

3.   Shortly after he took our advice and rented an off-street parking space.

4.   The Missouri summers were hot and humid; the winters cold and damp.

5.   Underneath the bridge creaked ominously.

28.10 AVOIDING COMMA ERRORS

Directions: In each of the following sentences, delete any unnecessary commas and add any that are needed.

Example: Bob excused himself, and hastily left the room.

A.   The ribbed vault, the flying buttress, and the pointed arch, are characteristic of Gothic architecture.

B.   Sometimes, the cost of meals, purchased during business trips, can be deducted from taxable income.

C.   The investigator was surprised to discover that the front door was locked, and that an alarm system had been installed.

D.   The city hopes that construction of the new hospital will be completed, before the college students return, in the fall.

E.   In the American justice system, a defendant is considered innocent, until proven guilty.

1.   The researcher, who designed the study, reported her conclusions in this month's volume of *Nature*.

2.   We couldn't help thinking, that your responses to our questions seemed rehearsed.

3.   The maitre d' welcomed regular customers with a polite, understated, bow, and unfamiliar diners with a curt smile.

4.   Louise's garden contained many flowering plants such as, tulips, gardenias, petunias and pansies.

5.   There is far too much pepper in this soup, but not enough onion.

28.11 REVIEW EXERCISE 1: USING COMMAS CORRECTLY

Directions: Edit the following paragraph to correct all errors in the use of commas.

A.   Samuel Johnson one of England's most colorful men of letters lived a life filled with contradictions. He was a scholarly man fluent in Greek Latin and French but he welcomed many poor uneducated people into his household. Although a deeply religious man he frequently suffered from religious doubts. He had a reputation for sloth yet he almost single-handedly compiled the first comprehensive English dictionary a remarkable feat when one considers that he was nearly blind as a result of a childhood case of scrofula. Although his contemporaries knew him as a poet an essayist and a brilliant conversationalist he is perhaps best remembered today as a lexicographer.

28.12 REVIEW EXERCISE 2: USING COMMAS CORRECTLY

Directions: Edit the following paragraph to correct all errors in the use of commas.

1. Well-known since Charles Darwin made them his laboratory in the 1830s the Galapagos Islands are famous for their giant tortoises and marine iguanas. Located some six hundred miles off the coast of Ecuador these islands still have secrets to unveil. Many of these are underwater however and explorers are just beginning to discover them. Darwin and his contemporaries only caught a glimpse of the undersea world through glass-bottomed buckets. Early in the next century divers donned scuba gear and descended as far as two hundred feet. At the end of that century intrepid divers used a small submersible to descend more than 1500 feet. The cold dark world they entered was teeming with life including squid sea cucumbers sharks goosefish and transparent eels. A series of dives yielded a dozen new species of vertebrate animals. A laboratory for Darwin the Galapagos it seems still have much to reveal.

    Adapted from John F. Ross, "IMAX Takes Us
    Undersea in the Galapagos," *Smithsonian* 30.7
    (1999): 52–64.

29.1   USING SEMICOLONS

Directions: In each of the following sentences, add semicolons or change commas to semicolons when necessary.

Example:

Original sentence: Betty had studied diligently for weeks, therefore, she did well on the history exam.

Revision: Betty had studied diligently for weeks; therefore, she did well on the history exam.

A.   To unwind after our final exam, we spent the evening watching a marathon of old romantic movies: *The Philadelphia Story,* starring Katharine Hepburn, Cary Grant, and James Stewart, *Roman Holiday,* with Audrey Hepburn and Gregory Peck, and the all-time classic *Casablanca,* with Humphrey Bogart and Ingrid Bergman.

B.   Water shortages are a serious problem in this area, consequently, many restaurants now only serve water when customers specifically request it.

C.   When parents look for good day-care services, they must consider the reputation of the provider, the size, location, and quality of the facilities, and the ratio of staff members to children.

D.   In 1900, the average life expectancy for an American was 47.3 years, by 1975, this average had increased to 72.4 years.

E.   Some specimens of the bristlecone pine are more than 4,000 years old this extreme age makes them the oldest living things on Earth.

1.   The most highly paid butlers, whose annual salaries exceed $50,000, are knowledgeable about food, wine, and formal etiquette, capable of managing and supervising large household staffs, and gifted with discreet, diplomatic temperaments.

2.   It snowed very little that winter nevertheless, sales of ski equipment were brisk.

3.   The cousins came from Albuquerque, New Mexico, Pace, Florida, Harrisonburg, Virginia, and Montgomery, Alabama, for the family reunion.

4.   Czar Peter the Great was a tall man, in fact, he stood nearly seven feet tall.

5.   Most people associate boomerangs with Australia however, ancient boomerangs have been discovered in every inhabited continent except South America.

29.2 USING COLONS

Directions: Edit each of the following sentences by adding, removing, or substituting colons for other punctuation marks.

Example:

Original sentence: Ned had only one reason for living in such a barren place, a very high salary.

Revised sentence: Ned had only one reason for living in such a barren place: a very high salary.

A. For his birthday Martin wanted: new running shoes, some video games, and a stopwatch.

B. Over vacation I read *Hardcore Troubadour: The Life and Near Death of Steve Earle.*

C. To restore company profits, the consultant recommended three actions; cut employee wages, increase advertising, and eliminate stock options.

D. Many theaters find that an 815 curtain time results in fewer latecomers than one at 800.

E. Two anticipated effects of the storm were: increased erosion of the shoreline and a flash flood in the center of town.

1. We needed to buy these ingredients to finish making the Christmas fruitcake, diced apricots, figs, molasses, brown sugar, and dried pears.

2. The airline serves many Asian cities, including: Tokyo, Beijing, Hong Kong, Singapore, and Seoul.

3. The movie had a disappointing ending; the hero joined the villains.

4. Before the 1600s, all carrots were one of these colors red, purple, or black.

5. The boys outnumbered the girls on the soccer team 3–1.

29.3 USING HYPHENS

Directions: In each of the following sentences, add hyphens where they are needed and delete them where they are not needed.

Example:

Original sentence: Sam wore his favorite Tshirt at the post game celebration.

Revised sentence: Sam wore his favorite T-shirt at the post-game celebration.

A. In keeping with the newly-established regulations, this facility is now scent-free.

B. Don't try to recreate the entire program; just do the best that you can.

C. Three quarters of the way through the exam, I realized that I didn't know enough about
    postReconstruction America to answer the last essay question.

D. Mother received a beautifully-embroidered shawl from her eldest daughter and some scented soaps
    from her sister in law.

E. Molly had always resented Marlin's devil may care attitude.

1. Please double space when typing your answers and leave one inch margins on all sides of the paper.

2. Jake's fear of heights was well-known, but he most dreaded looking down while riding on a really-
    steep escalator.

3. Jackson's Hardware was a store for do it yourself homeowners; Derek, the fix it man, loved it.

4. Because it didn't receive the all important high ratings, the new sitcom was canceled after only
    twenty four episodes.

5. The bamboo blinds came in three, four, and six foot sizes.

29.4   USING DASHES

Directions: Add dashes where they are needed in each of the following sentences.

Example:

Original sentence: There are two things that you should do eat less and exercise more to lose weight.

Edited sentence: There are two things that you should do—eat less and exercise more—to lose weight.

A.   This part of the report is important at least to me so pay attention.

B.   The most common means of evaluation the intelligence test is no longer considered sufficient as the sole indicator for determining whether to place students in a special education class.

C.   The northern New England states Maine, New Hampshire, and Vermont are likely to experience fuel shortages if this is a cold winter.

D.   Several of the professors I can't recall all of their names right now signed the petition.

E.   Some presidents John F. Kennedy, for example seem larger than life in the backward glance of historical perspective.

1.   Several features narrow handmade tires, sophisticated derailleurs, and lightweight alloy framing distinguish modern racing bicycles.

2.   Cheating, tardiness, rudeness none of these will be tolerated in this class.

3.   The key on the mantle why didn't I think of this earlier? should open the secret door.

4.   While in the Boston area we visited four historical places North Bridge, Lexington Green, Bunker Hill, and Old North Church related to the start of the Revolutionary War.

5.   The first speaker described one phenomenon jogging that she believes reflects many contemporary values.

29.5   USING SEMICOLONS, COLONS, AND DASHES

Directions: In each of the following sentences, insert the punctuation mark (semicolon, colon, or dash) that is most appropriate.

Example:

Original sentence: The city planners needed only one thing to make the project a success money.

Edited sentence: The city planners need only one thing to make the project a success—money.

A.   We saw a hastily scrawled note on the cabin door that let us know we weren't welcome NO VISITORS.

B.   Victims of Hurricane Katrina can use any basic supplies that you can spare food, water, clothing, medicine, or blankets.

C.   The thief's plan was obvious break the window, cut the wires, snatch the jewels, and climb down the fire escape.

D.   The project seemed like it would never end it lasted a week longer than scheduled.

E.   The experiment addressed the following effects of sleep deprivation listlessness, irritability, and the inability to concentrate.

1.   Altricial birds, woodpeckers, and hummingbirds these are all blind and almost featherless at birth.

2.   The president is going to veto the tax bill at least he said he would.

3.   Five suspicious passengers all without luggage were asked to leave the airplane before takeoff.

4.   Most car accidents have a single cause driver carelessness.

5.   Omar was ready to leave for his interview, but there was one small problem he couldn't find his car keys.

29.6   USING PARENTHESES AND BRACKETS

Directions: In each of the following sentences, insert parentheses or brackets where they are needed.

Example:

Original sentence: Only one variety of artichoke purple grows on the steepest hills.

Edited sentence: Only one variety of artichoke (purple) grows on the steepest hills.

A.   The coded message read, "Tell the boss Senator Butler that the eagle the German ambassador has landed."

B.   Some options for savers mutual funds, tax-exempt bonds, and zero-coupon bonds are not understood by many consumers.

C.   The term *gross national product GNP* refers to the total value of goods and services that a country produces in one year.

D.   "I have now reviewed the evidance sic," said the attorney, "and I believe that I can defend you properly."

E.   Descriptions may be *objective* focusing on the object itself or *subjective* focusing on the individual's response to the object.

1.   AARP American Association of Retired People is very active in defending senior citizens' rights.

2.   "This *stele* a commemorative stone tablet dates from the eighth century B.C.," explained the museum guide.

3.   The agronomist considered soybeans the crop of the future because 1 they are hearty, 2 they are high in protein, and 3 they require relatively small amounts of expensive fertilizer.

4.   Shirley Chisholm the country's first African American congresswoman used the campaign slogan "Unbought and Unbossed."

5.   "That was the year 1978 that we began manufacturing computer parts overseas," the executive told the board members.

29.7 USING APOSTROPHES

Directions: In each of the following sentences, insert any necessary apostrophes and delete any unnecessary ones. You may need to change the spelling of some words.

Example:

Original sentence: Daneesh kept pulling the yellow cats' tail.

Edited sentence: Daneesh kept pulling the yellow cat's tail.

A.   The mechanics estimate was lower than those of his' competitors, so I took you're advice and had him fix my car.

B.   While Joe was waiting in his boss' office, he reviewed Lawrence and Emily's attendance records.

C.   The childrens' clothing was soaked from the unexpected downpours'.

D.   I received three As and two Bs on my report card, so my grades were higher than anyone elses' in the class.

E.   Ill sew the costumes if youll paint the sets.

1.   Most of an attorneys day—from eight oclock until two oclock—is spent in hearing's, committee meetings, and court sessions; he or she must also review clients cases during these hours'.

2.   My sister-in-laws house is more than 150 years old; its most interesting feature is a hidden passageway in the library.

3.   Theres a tavern down the road where many residents' of the mountain villages gather at the days' end.

4.   "Who's muddy shoes are these?" asked Samanthas mother.

5.   Are you going to Karen's and Alphonse's house for dinner tomorrow?

29.8   USING QUOTATION MARKS—SET 1

Directions: Correctly punctuate each of the following items by adding or deleting quotation marks and any other punctuation and by changing letters to uppercase or lowercase. Begin a new paragraph when one is needed.

Example:

Original sentence: Did you buy oysters, asked Melba?

Edited sentence: "Did you buy oysters?" asked Melba.

A.   Why were we assigned Doris Lessing's story The Old Chief Mshlanga?

B.   Sonya in Chekhov's *Uncle Vanya* says, When a woman isn't beautiful, people always say, "You have lovely eyes[;] you have lovely hair."

C.   One small step for [a] man, one giant step for mankind, Neil Armstrong said as he set foot on the moon in July 1969.

D.   The novel's first chapter, A Tortuous Beginning, was so confusing that I refused to continue reading.

E.   "Look out," Manuel exclaimed! "That big boulder is headed your way".

1.   English poet William Blake wrote, I must Create a System or be enslaved by another Man's.

2.   The judge asked the members of the jury "whether they had reached a verdict."

3.   Benjamin Disraeli, British prime minister during part of Queen Victoria's long reign, once said, There are lies, damned lies, and statistics.

4.   Had you read Hemingway's story "A Clean, Well-Lighted Place" before writing your term paper, asked the teacher?

5.   Did you know that some of the officers in the American Revolution came to this country from Poland specifically to help us win the war asked the history instructor. Our town, Pulaski, Tennessee, is named for one of them a student answered. Correct that was Count Casimir Pulaski responded the teacher.

29.9   USING QUOTATION MARKS—SET 2

Directions: Correctly punctuate the following items by adding or deleting quotation marks or any other punctuation marks and by changing letters to uppercase or lowercase. Begin a new paragraph when one is needed.

Example:

Original sentence: Are you familiar with the Derek and the Dominoes version of "Little Wing?"

Edited sentence: Are you familiar with the Derek and the Dominoes version of "Little Wing"?

A.   I think that I shall never see / a billboard as lovely as a tree, wrote Ogden Nash in a parody of Joyce Kilmer's poem Trees.

B.   When did Howard Stern start referring to himself as the King of All Media?

C.   Who said, "You can't step in the same river twice," asked the philosophy professor?

D.   "Give me different mothers", St. Augustine said, and I will give you a different world".

E.   Babe Ruth's amazing ability to hit home runs earned him the nickname Sultan of Swat.

1.   In his Nobel Peace Prize acceptance speech, Martin Luther King, Jr., said, I accept this award today with an abiding faith in America and an audacious faith in the future of mankind.

2.   What time is it? Kim asked. I don't know, Derrick replied, Has the alarm already gone off, she asked. I didn't hear it, he said.

3.   The article's title, The Ethics of Price Fixing, is sure to stimulate a response.

4.   In the poem Maud Muller, John Greenleaf Whittier wrote, For of all sad words of tongue or pen, / The saddest are these: "It might have been"!

5.   When you have finished reading the paper, Bruce said, Be sure to put it in the recycling bin.

29.10   USING ITALICS

Directions: In each of the following sentences, put the correct word or words in italics.

Example:

Original sentence: The word stuff can refer to almost anything.

Edited sentence: The word *stuff* can refer to almost anything.

A.   Lorry is the British word for truck.

B.   The French use the expression bon appetit at the beginning of a meal, but many Americans simply

say, "Enjoy."

C.   Charles Lindbergh flew solo across the Atlantic in The Spirit of St. Louis.

D.   The wat, or Buddhist temple, serves as the social and religious center of most Thai villages.

E.   Some people say they have encountered ghosts aboard the ocean liner Queen Mary.

1.   Like Americans, Brazilians love soap operas, which they call telenovas.

2.   Yes, I would say that arriving two days late for your interview is being extremely late.

3.   The common abbreviation a.m. stands for ante meridiem, a Latin phrase meaning "before noon."

4.   The tragic end of the space shuttle Columbia eroded the public's confidence in the shuttle program.

5.   People learning to pronounce English as a foreign language often have trouble with l's, g's, and k's.

29.11 PUNCTUATING TITLES

Directions: Add the necessary quotation marks or italics to the titles in the following sentences.

Example:

Original sentence: Unlike other newspapers, USA today is distributed nationwide.

Edited sentence: Unlike other newspapers, *USA Today* is distributed nationwide.

A. The first song on A Mighty Field of Vision, a CD anthology of the music of recently rediscovered soul singer Eddie Hinton, is I Got the Feeling.

B. Tim Robbins starred in Jacob's Ladder, a film that deals with a Vietnam veteran's frightening flashbacks.

C. The film Finding Neverland told how J. M. Barrie, played by Johnny Depp, came to write the play Peter Pan.

D. Gabriel García Márquez, a Colombian-born, Nobel Prize–winning novelist, wrote One Hundred Years of Solitude.

E. The poem Video Cuisine appears in Maxine Kumin's collection The Long Approach.

1. The film Brokeback Mountain is based on E. Annie Proulx's short story Brokeback Mountain.

2. The Rolling Stones' song Sweet Virginia is on their classic album Exile on Main Street.

3. For more than two hundred years, George Frederick Handel's Messiah has been a favorite piece of Christmas music.

4. This month's issue of Vanity Fair has an article about New York Times reporters who fabricated sources.

5. Some television viewers tune in to Washington Week in Review for political commentary; others prefer to get it on The Daily Show.

29.12 USING ELLIPSIS POINTS

Directions: Each of the following items represents unfinished thoughts or incorporates part of a quotation into a sentence or sentences. Rewrite each of the following items by punctuating the italicized words (and the spaces around and between them) appropriately; by capitalizing or lowercasing letters; and by using dashes, parentheses, brackets, slashes, and ellipsis points as needed. The entire quotation used for each item is contained in bold brackets. You are to incorporate part of the quotation into the sentence or sentences by using correct punctuation and capitalization.

Example:

Material to be presented with ellipsis points:

John Steinbeck wrote to a friend about visiting Camelot: "Yesterday I climbed Camelot on a golden *day. We* could see the Bristol Channel and Glastonbury too, and King Alfred's tower and all below. And that wonderful place and structure with layer on layer of work and feeling. I found myself weeping."

[*Entire quotation:* "Yesterday I climbed Camelot on a golden day. The orchards are in flower and we could see the Bristol Channel and Glastonbury too, and King Alfred's tower and all below. And that wonderful place and structure with layer on layer of work and feeling. I found myself weeping."]

John Steinbeck, letter to Eugène Vinaver, 1959.

Revised passage using ellipsis points to indicate omission:

John Steinbeck wrote to a friend about visiting Camelot: "Yesterday I climbed Camelot on a golden day. . . . We could see the Bristol Channel and Glastonbury too, and King Alfred's tower and all below. And that wonderful place and structure with layer on layer of work and feeling. I found myself weeping."

John Steinbeck, letter to Eugène Vinaver, 1959.

A.   Ursula Le Guin believes:

Science fiction is the mythology of the modern world—or one of its *mythologies—For* science fiction does use the mythmaking faculty to apprehend the world we live in, a world profoundly shaped and changed by science and technology; and its originality is that it uses the mythmaking faculty on new material.

[***Entire quotation:*** "Science fiction is the mythology of the modern world—or one of its mythologies—even though it is a highly intellectual form of art, and mythology is a nonintellectual mode of apprehension. For science fiction does use the mythmaking faculty to apprehend the world we live in, a world profoundly shaped and changed by science and technology; and its originality is that it uses the mythmaking faculty on new material.]

> Ursula K. Le Guin, "Myth and Archetype in Science Fiction," in *The Language of the Night: Essays on Fantasy and Science Fiction*, ed. Susan Wood (New York: Berkley Books, 1982), 64.

B. How do we define *trash*? Susan Strasser maintains that we determine what we consider trash "by sorting. Everything that comes into the end-of-the-millennium *home eventually* requires a decision: keep it or toss it. We use it up, we save it to use later, we give it away, or at some point we define it as rubbish, to be taken back out, removed beyond the borders of the household."

[***Entire quotation:*** "Trash is created by sorting. Everything that comes into the end-of-the millennium home—every toaster, pair of trousers, and ounce of soda pop, and every box and bag and bottle they arrive in—eventually requires a decision: keep it or toss it. We use it up, we save it to use later, we give it away, or at some point we define it as rubbish, to be taken back out, removed beyond the borders of the household."]

> Susan Strasser, *Waste and Want: A Social History of Trash* (New York: Holt, 1999), 5.

C. Hugh Howard tells us that "Determining the vintage of a house is more than a matter of chronology. Establishing the year in which it was constructed is just a starting *point in* understanding and appreciating a house."

[*Entire quotation:* "Determining the vintage of a house is more than a matter of chronology. Establishing the year in which it was constructed is just a starting point (and not the only one) in understanding and appreciating a house."]

Hugh Howard, *How Old Is This House?* (New York: Noonday Press/Farrar, 1989), xiii.

D. Although most people associate epic poems such as Homer's *The Iliad* and *The Odyssey* with the poetry of ancient Greece, there were also shorter poems created "For private occasions, and particularly to entertain guests at the cultivated drinking parties known as *symposia. These* poems were often full of passion, whether love or hatred, and could be personal or, often, highly political."

[*Entire quotation:* "For private occasions, and particularly to entertain guests at the cultivated drinking parties known as *symposia*, shorter poetic forms were developed. These poems were often full of passion, whether love or hatred, and could be personal or, often, highly political."]

The Greek Islands, ed. Isabel Carlisle et al. (New York: DK Publishing, 1998), 54.

E. In Stephen Crane's short story "The Blue Hotel," the action develops as one of the hotel guests, the paranoid Swede, loses control of himself as he gets drunk:

At six-o'clock supper, the Swede fizzed like a fire-wheel. He sometimes seemed on the point of bursting into riotous song, and in all his madness he was encouraged by old *Scully*. The Swede domineered the whole feast, and he gave it the appearance of a crude bacchanal. He seemed to have grown suddenly taller; he gazed, brutally disdainful, into every face. His voice rang through the room.

[*Entire quotation:* "At six-o'clock supper, the Swede fizzed like a fire-wheel. He sometimes seemed on the point of bursting into riotous song, and in all his madness he was encouraged by old Scully. The Easterner was encased in reserve; the cowboy sat in wide-mouthed amazement, forgetting to eat, while Johnnie wrathfully demolished great plates of food. The daughters of the house, when they were obliged to replenish the biscuits, approached as warily as Indians, and, having succeeded in their purpose, fled with ill-concealed trepidation. The Swede domineered the whole feast, and he gave it the appearance of a crude bacchanal. He seemed to have grown suddenly taller; he gazed, brutally disdainful, into every face. His voice rang through the room."]

Stephen Crane, "The Blue Hotel," in *The Red Badge of Courage and Other Stories*, ed. Richard Chase (Boston: Houghton Mifflin, 1960), 263.

1.   In her last speech to her husband, Torvald, Nora declares her independence: "I'm freeing you from being *responsible. There* has to be absolute freedom for us both."

[*Entire quotation:* "I'm freeing you from being responsible. Don't feel yourself bound, any more than I will. There has to be absolute freedom for us both."]

Henrik Ibsen, *A Doll's House*, 64.

2.   **Directions:** Represent unfinished thoughts in the following item:

I'm not *sure I'm* not *understanding help* me out here!

3.   Walt Whitman mourns the death of Abraham Lincoln in the poem beginning with these famous lines: "O *Captain! the* prize we sought is won."

[*Entire quotation:*

O Captain! my Captain! our fearful trip is done,

The ship has weather'd every rack, the prize we sought is won.]

4.   In "Guinevere," Tennyson writes:

    After the sunset down the coast, he heard

    Strange music, and he paused and *turning*

    He saw them—headland after headland flame

    Far into the rich heart of the west.

[*Entire quotation:*

After the sunset down the coast, he heard

Strange music, and he paused and turning—there,

All down the lonely coast of Lyonesse,

Each with a beacon-star upon his head,

And with a wild sea-light about his feet,

He saw them—headland after headland flame

Far into the rich heart of the west.]

                      Alfred Tennyson, "Guinevere."

5.   De Quincey tells us: "Had it been possible for the world to measure [Miss Smith] by her powers, rather than by her performances, she would have been *placed at* the head of learned women."

[*Entire quotation:* "Miss Smith was really a most extraordinary person. . . . Had it been possible for the world to measure her by her powers, rather than by her performances, she would have been placed, perhaps in the estimate of posterity, at the head of learned women."]

                      Thomas De Quincey, "Society of the Lakes."

30.1   CAPITALIZING FIRST WORDS

Directions: Edit each of the following sentences for correct capitalization of first words. If there are no errors in a sentence, write "Correct."

Example:

Original sentence: One type of blueberry is native to the Deep South: The rabbit-eye.

Edited sentence: One type of blueberry is native to the Deep South: the rabbit-eye.

A.   When did Mae West say, "too much of a good thing can be wonderful"?

B.   "You can have some dessert," Aunt Lucy told the children, "If you behave yourselves."

C.   There's only one explanation for the Enron executives' actions: Greed.

D.   Robert said, "Let's review this material one more time."

E.   We will drive you to the train station (First we will have to figure out where it is) and then go grocery shopping.

1.   Children always delight in hearing these words from the most widely read editorial in the history of the *New York Sun:* "Yes, Virginia, there is a Santa Claus."

2.   Kent finally told us why he moved to rural Nevada: property values were lower there.

3.   Clarence was awarded first prize in the bake-off for his pineapple upside-down cake. (some people thought that Zelda's prune soufflé deserved the honor.)

4.   In "The House of Silence," Thomas Hardy wrote these lines about Max Gate: "That is a quiet place— / that house in the trees with the shady lawn."

5.   Your emergency pack should include (1) Candles, (2) Batteries, (3) a Blanket, and (4) Water.

30.2   CAPITALIZING PROPER NOUNS

Directions: Edit each of the following sentences for correct capitalization of proper nouns.

Example:

Original sentence: I enjoyed taking the Russian History course.

Edited sentence: I enjoyed taking the Russian history course.

A.   More than seven hundred years ago, the anasazi people of the American southwest built cliff

dwellings that continue to amaze visitors today.

B.   F. Scott Fitzgerald's story "The diamond as big as the Ritz" contains a theme that would reappear in

the great Gatsby.

C.   Maurice advised us to drive North for several hours before heading east on I-80.

D.   I have to take English Literature, World History, and Calculus 101 to complete my graduation

requirements.

E.   The norman conquest of England, led by William the conqueror, began in 1066.

1.   Works such as *el jaleo, lady with the rose,* and *gassed* helped make John Singer Sargent one of the

most popular painters of the Twentieth Century.

2.   I asked my Mother if she still had the old family bible.

3.   John Edwards, former Senator from north Carolina, now works for a foundation combating poverty

in the south.

4.   Mark Gifford, who holds a Doctor of Philosophy degree, will be the guest lecturer in history 305

today.

5.   Robin was invited to participate in the artists for peace lecture series at the University.

30.3 CAPITALIZING OTHER WORDS

Directions: Edit each of the following sentences for correct use of capital letters.

Example:

Original sentence: The Mayor of Detroit was the featured speaker at the Memorial Day Ceremony.

Edited sentence: The mayor of Detroit was the featured speaker at the Memorial Day ceremony.

A.   Jamal moved to the south because he could no longer deal with winters in the northeast.

B.   Barbara would rather post humorous family pictures on her web site than send them in the U.S. Mail.

C.   Harold Born, Senior Vice President, has worked for the company for twenty years.

D.   The republican party was known as the antislavery party at the time of the civil war.

E.   Some Conservatives consider those who opposed the invasion of Iraq to be Un-American.

1.   Akhenaton, who was first known as Amenhotep, ruled Ancient Egypt until his death in 1358 b.c.e.

2.   Ralph has made more business contacts on the internet than he has through his job at the State University.

3.   The letter was addressed to capt. Ross Bingaman, who had been a Senior Officer at Pease Air Force base during the Vietnam war.

4.   LuAnn had attended a Northern Illinois College before transferring to a business school last Fall.

5.   It's legal to make a u-turn in california, but don't try to make one in this state.

31.1   SPOTTING MISSPELLED WORDS

Directions: Correct any spelling errors that you find in the following sentences.

received   *beautiful*
Example: Daniel ~~recieved~~ an award for his ~~beautifull~~ painting.

A.   Louise and I always end up in an arguement when we start discussing politics.

B.   Desmond perfered staying home and listening to classical music while his twin brother Brent enjoyed

hearing loud rock bands at smoke-filed clubs.

C.   Russell's judgement was impairred when he hadn't had enough sleep.

D.   We realy enjoyed visiting the zebras and the monkies at the San Diego Zoo.

E.   Brad was truley sorry about the dreadfull condition of the driveway.

1.   We were just begining to understand the poem when the poet began using more complicated

imagry.

2.   Not even his freinds believe his excuses.

3.   The New Orleans chef was serving fryed catfish and blackenned salmon in the formal dining room.

4.   Our seventh-grade teacher always told us that when we hurryed, we misspeled too many words.

5.   There were ninty-five applicants for the position at the haulling company.

31.2 FORMING PLURALS

Directions: Correct any spelling errors that you find in the following sentences. If a sentence contains no errors, write "Correct."

Example: This Mexican restaurant serves wonderful enchiladas, ~~burritoes~~ *burritos*, and ~~tacoes~~ *tacos*.

A. The two music stores compete to offer the lowest prices for their CDs'.

B. The childrens' parents had packed their lunchs before sending them off on the hike.

C. Henry VIII had two of his six wifes executed.

D. Gilda and Helen received their Ph.D.'s in cultural anthropology last year.

E. The doctor told me to put two spoonfulls of honey in my tea and to take my vitamines every morning.

1. The musicians brought their banjoes, mandolins, and guitars to the folk festival.

2. We heard the echos of the horses' hoofs as the herd thundered through the canyon.

3. Jim grew garlic, onions, herbes, and tomatoes in his garden.

4. The waitress served three Bloody Marys to the men at the table by the windows.

5. Five of my sisters and two of my brother-in-laws are staying with us for the family reunion.

31.3   REVIEW EXERCISE: SPELLING

Directions: Correct any spelling errors that you find in the following sentences.

radios
Example: Robert collects Bakelite ~~radioes~~ from the 1940s.

A.   The barnyard was a scene of chaos with sheep, horses, gooses, and goats all runing loose.

B.   The carpenters were useing thinner pieces of paneling because they were more pliable.

C.   Our new nieghbors brought us some lettuce, tomatos, and dryed herbs from their organic garden.

D.   Because the college's enrollement keeps increasing, more dormitories must be built.

E.   Some very wierd occurences have been reported at that deserted beach.

1.   The maids of honor were releived to see the bride stop hesitatting and start walking down the aisle.

2.   The attornies advised the suspect to think carefully before making a statment to the police.

3.   The heros of the battle said that they had only been fulfiling their duties as paratroopers.

4.   The ancient Greeks believed that gods and godesses controlled their fates.

5.   Elizabeth Taylor has had some cameoes in some forgettible films lately.

32.1 WRITING OR SPELLING NUMBERS

Directions: Correct any errors in the use of numbers in the following sentences. If numbers are correctly written as numerals or spelled out in a sentence, write "Correct."

Example: The contestants ranged in age from *eight* ~~8~~ to twelve years old.

A. LaRue estimated that fifteen percent of the class had failed the quiz.

B. To get ready for the big race, Henry ran 3 miles one day, 5 miles the second day, and 8 miles the next.

C. We purchased ten three-pound packages of chicken for the barbeque.

D. The average grade on the calculus test was sixty-two before the professor applied the curve.

E. We couldn't believe that it cost 40 dollars to attend the 2-hour concert.

1. Larry didn't arrive at the bus station until 4 o'clock.

2. Mrs. Monaghan has lived at thrity-five Foster Avenue all of her life.

3. We counted twenty seven sailboats on the lake yesterday afternoon and forty five today.

4. 12 people showed up at the raffle with winning tickets.

5. After three periods the hockey playoff game was tied seven to seven, and the teams were headed into overtime.

32.2   USING ABBREVIATIONS AND ACRONYMS

Directions: In each of the following sentences, correct any errors in the use of abbreviations or acronyms. If a sentence is correct, write "Correct."

New York City

Example: Some tourists are overwhelmed by the size of ~~NYC~~.

A.   We saw many amazing animals—elephant seals, otters, sea lions, pelicans, etc.—on our trip to

Monterey Bay.

B.   The F.B.I., the C.I.A., and F.E.M.A. aren't held in the highest regard by the American public.

C.   Uncle Steve moved from Reno, NV, to Huntsville, AL, last year.

D.   Martha Stewart has a good recipe for dumplings on pg. 9 of her latest cookbook.

E.   We measured the plot in meters, not in yds.

1.   Retail sales rose more than 15% between Nov. and Dec.

2.   Most people have traded their V.C.R.s for D.V.D. players, and rental stores have encouraged the

trend by phasing out rentals of videotapes.

3.   My superstitious sister's birthday, Oct. 13, will fall on a Fri. this year.

4.   Semiramis, who may have built the Hanging Gardens of Babylon, ruled Assyria from 811 to 808

BCE.

5.   We caught forty lbs. of fish & then sailed home.

32.3   REVIEW EXERCISE: NUMBERS, ABBREVIATIONS, CAPITALS, AND APOSTROPHES

Directions: In each of the following paragraphs, correct all errors in capitalization, abbreviations, apostrophes, and the use of numbers.

A.   One of the greatest dangers facing space travelers today is a swarm of human-made particles orbiting the earth. 106 particles struck the space shuttle *columbia* on one of it's missions. In an effort to avoid these dangerous projectiles, the U.S. space command, located in Colorado Springs, CO, tracks every piece of space junk that is any larger than two-and-one-half inches in diameter. At present, there are about 9,000 pieces of debris this size in orbit around the earth. Some of these are moving dangerously fast, up to 17,000 m.p.h. At this speed, a projectile that weighs one oz. can create an 18-in. hole in a sheet of steel that is 1 inch thick. Researchers' continue to work on creating better armor plating for spacecraft, but avoiding contact with the deadly particles is the best way to avoid disaster.

> Adapted from James R. Chiles, "Casting a High-Tech Net for Space Junk," *Smithsonian* 29.10 (1999): 46–55.

1.   Under an ancient calendar, the Roman's observed Mar. twenty-five, the beginning of spring, as the 1st day of the year. Emperors and high-ranking officials, though, repeatedly tampered with the length of months and days to extend their terms of office. Calendar dates were so desynchronized with astronomical benchmarks by the year 153 b.c. that the roman senate, to set many public occasions straight, declared the start of the New Year as Jan. 1. However, more tampering again set dates askew. To reset the calendar to Jan. 1 in forty-six B.C., Julius Caesar had to let the year drag on for four hundred and forty-five days, earning it the historical sobriquet "Year of Confusion." Caesars new calendar was eponymously called the julian calendar.

> Charles Panati, *Extraordinary Origins of Everyday Things* (New York: Harper, 1987), 46–47.

PART 8
MULTILINGUAL AND
ESL GUIDELINES

34.1 COUNT AND NONCOUNT NOUNS

Directions: In the following sentences, correct any errors in the use of count and noncount nouns. If a sentence is correct, write "Correct."

Example: ~~The~~ Honesty is the best policy in business dealings.

A. Dog across the street was howling all night.

B. Eric will study the physics in graduate school next year.

C. Henrietta's favorite vegetable is spinach.

D. Northern Washington State has a lovely scenery.

E. John is hoping to find the employment in the service industry.

1. We heard a thunder in the distance as we drove home.

2. Jane taught me how to make the recipe for apple fritters.

3. College students often drink the strong coffee when studying for exams.

4. Brent gave me an advice about fixing my computer.

5. The wood is often used for constructing houses in warm climates.

34.2   ARTICLES AND POSSESSIVE AND DEMONSTRATIVE ADJECTIVES

Directions: Edit the following sentences for correct use of articles and possessive and demonstrative adjectives.

Example: We visited ~~the~~ Washington, D.C., last spring.

A.   The line of tourists at a White House was already quite long, winding along a street next to White House lawn called the Ellipse.

B.   I walked around an Ellipse and up small hill to a Washington Monument.

C.   A line there was not as long, so I waited under a circle of the fifty flags, one for every state in a United States.

D.   From an information in mine guidebook, I learned that this monument is 555 feet tall and was a tallest structure in world when it was built in the 1886.

E.   After climbing to observation area at a top of a monument, I could see all of the Washington area spread out before me.

1.   Across grassy area called a Mall, I could see a Capitol Building and the some museums.

2.   Toward a west I could see a monument to the President Lincoln, toward an east the monument to President Jefferson.

3.   Beyond that two monuments was a meandering Potomac River.

4.   When I came down from a monument, I realized that there was much more a distance between buildings than I had thought when viewing them from up high.

5.   I also realized that I would be doing a great deal of the walking in a city before the end of a day.

34.3 Showing Quantities of Nouns

Directions: Edit the following sentences so that they correctly express quantities of nouns.

Example: The tourists saw ~~the~~ fifteen pelicans on the wharf.

A. Mother bought plenty of the groceries to feed the guests.

B. However, she forgot bag of flour at the checkout counter.

C. The butcher told her that a several kinds of beef were good.

D. He also recommended buying the some fish fillets.

E. Now we have the many choices of foods for dinner.

1. Janice is sending the twenty-five people invitations to the party.

2. She expects that the few won't be able to attend.

3. A many of the guests said that they would bring refreshments.

4. The both of her upstairs neighbors offered to help decorate the living room.

5. The number of other people said that they would bring a some music videos.

34.4   PROGRESSIVE VERBS AND VERB COMPLEMENTS

Directions: Edit the following sentences so that they have the correct form of a progressive verb or use the correct form of the linking verb *be* with complements.

Example: Tom is ~~being~~ my chemistry lab partner this semester.

A.   The plane take off as the rain began to fall.

B.   I was being sick all last week.

C.   John is knowing how to return to the campsite.

D.   She still looked for her glasses when the movie started.

E.   They be eating lunch in the kitchen now.

1.   The cook was toss the salad while the rolls burned.

2.   Julian is being nervous about reading his essay to the class.

3.   Claire and Eustis learn how to play the piano.

4.   Lyndon B. Johnson was being president of the United States during the Vietnam War.

5.   We think about you when you telephoned us last night.

34.5   VERBS FOLLOWED BY GERUNDS AND INFINITIVES

Directions: Edit the following sentences so that they contain the correct form of the gerund or infinitive.

to go

Example: We wanted ~~going~~ to the Rolling Stones concert.

A.   Don't delay to send your money for the tickets.

B.   I now remember to leave my sweater at your house last night.

C.   We wanted learning more about the Spanish Inquisition in history class.

D.   I will not deny to run the red light, but I hope that the police officer didn't notice me.

E.   Luis persuaded his mother allowing him to borrow the family car for the weekend.

1.   When Marya visited the Sahara Desert, she could not imagine to be in a hotter place.

2.   Hank stopped to eat dairy products when he became a vegan.

3.   Habib remembered removing the safety latch before he used the power tool.

4.   Jim enjoyed to surf the huge waves during the high tides.

5.   The store manager authorized the clerk exchanging the defective speakers that I had purchased for

new ones.

34.6   MODAL VERBS

Directions: In the blank in each sentence, write the correct form of the verb contained in the brackets, preceded by an appropriate modal auxiliary verb or verbs. Use the meaning suggested in the brackets as a guide.

Example: He *will study* [*study*; intention] his math problems tonight.

A.   If I had written to you sooner, you _____ [*know*; speculation] about the delay in our travel plans.

B.   I _____ [*wash*; necessity] the floor before my guests arrive.

C.   When we went to the beach every summer, we _____ [*build*; repeated action] huge sand castles every day.

D.   We _____ [*finish*; necessity] fertilizing the lawn before it rains.

E.   Myrtle said she _____ [*go*; possibility] to Florida this winter.

1.   If we had known that you were coming for dinner, we _____ [*set*; speculation] an extra place at the table.

2.   Karen wasn't on the plane that just landed; she _____ [*be*; possibility or logical assumption] on the next one.

3.   Dan is never on time for anything; we _____ [*know*; expectation] that he would be late for the performance.

4.   You _____ [*take*; possibility] the mountain road home if the weather isn't too foggy.

5.   The football team _____ [*win*; possibility] the state championship if it wins the next two games.

34.7   TWO-WORD VERBS

Directions: In each of the following sentences, write in the blank the word or words that complete the verb.

Example: Sheila is just getting <u>over</u> the flu.

A.   John's old car often breaks _____ on long trips.

B.   Michelle picked _____ the nectarines without bruises at the farm stand.

C.   Don't put _____ until tomorrow what you can do today.

D.   I could not figure _____ how to solve the math problem.

E.   You must hang _____ the phone before you can receive a fax.

1.   Louise is trying _____ the dress that she ordered from the catalog.

2.   All class members should write _____ their seating preferences on these slips of

     paper.

3.   Because it was raining so hard, we had to call _____ the company picnic.

4.   I will have to think your proposal _____ carefully before I respond.

5.   Jane will look that information _____ for you in the faculty directory.

34.8 FORMING CORRECT VERB TENSES

Directions: Edit each of the following sentences for correct use of *-d* and *-ed* verb endings.

Example: When I turn**ed** the corner, I realized that I was on the wrong street.

A. Before I registered for an 8 a.m. class, I use to sleep until noon.

B. Rosalie nervously smooth the wrinkles of her dress before returning for her encore.

C. Our office change to a new computer system last month, but most of the employees haven't figured

out how to operate it yet.

D. I felt oblige to attend Raoul's poetry reading although I really don't like his poetry.

E. Books began falling to the floor when I move the bookshelf away from the wall.

1. When I listen to the CD a few more times, I didn't like it as well as I had the first time that I

heard it.

2. Every time Bernie and Paul skied down Devil's Slide, they risk their lives.

3. We were surprise to see so many people at the outdoor concert in the cold drizzle.

4. Ted dream about owning a black dog; then one appear on his doorstep a few days later.

5. After eight hours the workers had accomplish their goal of painting the front of the house.

34.9   PLACEMENT OF ADJECTIVES

Directions: Edit the following sentences to make sure that adjectives are correctly placed and punctuated. If a sentence is correct, write "Correct."

Example: This is the |messy| |last| room that I'm going to clean!

A.   We are finally planning to replace the porcelain old avocado-colored sink in our rustic kitchen.

B.   Father Poulos plans the annual giant Greek Orthodox Easter picnic in the town largest park.

C.   When we went to the car dealership, we saw many red expensive cars, but we wanted a white inexpensive car.

D.   That was the Danish most depressing movie that I've ever seen!

E.   Evelyn forgot her huge new flowered umbrella on the bus.

1.   I'm looking forward to living in England, but I'm not looking forward to damp cold many days.

2.   A yellow small shed stands at the end of her wooden new walkway in the secluded garden.

3.   The baby's cozy room was painted a green pleasant color that reminded us of spring new leaves.

4.   The university named her an honorary doctor of humanities.

5.   Marcia lost her balance during her swim aerobics class and got a purple enormous bruise on her shoulder.

34.10 PARTICIPLES AND NOUNS AS ADJECTIVES

Directions: Edit the following sentences so that they contain the correct forms of participles or nouns used as adjectives.

surprised

Example: Louise had a ~~surprising~~ look on her face when we all arrived for her birthday party.

A.   The thrilled end of the ballgame made us all go home feeling exhilarating.

B.   I am always annoying when she tells those bored stories about her childhood.

C.   Denise must pay a well-deserving fine for returning the libraries books so late.

D.   One of my most embarrassed moments was accidentally setting off the alarm one morning before the store was open.

E.   Ramon reluctantly brought his disappointed first-semester report card home to his waited parents.

1.   The worried director made her exhausting cast rehearse the play one more time.

2.   Veronica and Harold work as mails carriers.

3.   Tonight's algebra homework contains some of the most confused problems that I've ever seen.

4.   The stunning news editor watched in disbelief as the shocked news appeared on the computer screen.

5.   Michael's grandfather told a fascinated tale about life in the coals mines.

34.11   PLACEMENT OF ADVERBS

Directions: Revise each of the following sentences to show the correct placement of adverbs or prepositional phrases acting as adverbs. If a sentence is correct, write "Correct."

Example: He | remembers | seldom | his mother's birthday.

A.   My family around the block moved last year.

B.   Thomas asks never for help with his writing.

C.   That is the depressing most news I've heard in a long time.

D.   Claire near the fountain waited a long time for Kurt.

E.   We always eat lunch at that Thai restaurant on Tuesdays.

1.   John will tell us now our project assignments.

2.   It rains heavily usually in December in the Bay Area.

3.   The Burns family is late always for the meeting.

4.   A ring appears often around the moon before a storm.

5.   I will tomorrow arrive in Rome.

34.12   PREPOSITIONS AND PHRASAL PREPOSITIONS

Directions: In each of the following sentences, write the correct preposition or phrasal preposition in the blank.

Example: We jumped *into* the icy waters *of* the lake.

A.   Bob ordered fajitas _____ tacos.

B.   When the temperature falls _____ zero, I think _____ moving to a warmer climate.

C.   Meet me _____ 3 p.m. _____ the grocery store.

D.   I read _____ the Senate hearings _____ *Newsweek*.

E.   We took the mountain road _____ the severe weather warning.

1.   I found your street address _____ the campus directory.

2.   We traveled _____ Germany _____ our summer vacation.

3.   Return your completed application _____ March 13.

4.   Leon was sitting _____ the fire _____ the campsite.

5.   The dog was lying _____ the table waiting _____ us to put some dinner scraps _____ his bowl.

35.1   SENTENCE PATTERNS

Directions: Edit each of the following sentences to make sure that you have the correct word order. If a sentence is written correctly, write "Correct." Then label any of these sentence elements that appear in the sentence: **S** (subject), **AV** (active verb), **LV** (linking verb), **PA** (predicate adjective), **PN** (predicate nominative), **DO** (direct object), **IO** (indirect object), **OC** (object complement).

Example:

Original sentence: Lincoln gave some flowers Rosalba.

$$\text{S} \quad \text{AV} \quad \text{IO} \qquad \text{DO}$$

Revision with labels: Lincoln gave Rosalba some flowers.

A.   The court sent a subpoena the witness.

B.   Here are for you some letters.

C.   Sharon was short for someone her age.

D.   The waitress brought some soup the hungry customers.

E.   The meteorology students visited yesterday Mount Washington.

1.   Jesse Owens broke in his lifetime seven world records.

2.   A four-alarm fire was there on the next block.

3.   You are wearing that ugly coat why?

4.   Monteil the teacher considered the best student in the class.

5.   Mary the president of the physics club was.

35.2   DOUBLE NEGATIVES AND DOUBLE SUBJECTS

Directions: Edit the following sentences to eliminate any double negatives or double subjects.

Example: The clock ~~it~~ stopped working last night.

A.   The new video games they are very expensive.

B.   There are never no empty seats on the bus at rush hour.

C.   I forgot that your cousin he doesn't know my address.

D.   The dermatologist he gave my mother some lotion for her rash.

E.   We seldom don't get much mail.

1.   The teacher she gave us a long writing assignment.

2.   I don't never remember working on one this long before.

3.   After people they suffer a long illness, they may feel weak for months afterward.

4.   The house it was built in 1875.

5.   It is hardly not worth the time to travel all the way to the park in the late afternoon.

35.3   OMITTED WORDS

Directions: In each of the following sentences, supply the missing word or words.

Example:

Original sentence: Not very warm today.

Revised sentence: It is not very warm today.

A.   *War and Peace* is a very long novel; tells about Russia in the nineteenth century.

B.   As you know, are many Internet providers for e-mail.

C.   Pit bulls sometimes very dangerous animals.

D.   Healthy to get fresh air daily.

E.   Some rare paintings have been stolen from museums; can never be replaced.

1.   Your mother is flying to Virginia for Christmas; is excited about the trip.

2.   Many reasons to avoid eating much red meat.

3.   Many streets in San Francisco quite steep.

4.   When closed, most factory workers lost their jobs.

5.   Some groups protested the film's release because was so violent.

35.4   CONDITIONAL SENTENCES

Directions: In each of the following sentences, insert in the blank the appropriate form of the verb contained in the brackets. The context is also indicated in the brackets.

Example: If you swim with sharks, you *could be eaten* [*eat*; speculative].

A.   When the lake freezes over, ice fishermen _____ [*set*; factual] up their ice

   houses and wait for the fish to bite.

B.   Unless you have a lot of money, you _____ not

   _____ [*move*; predictive] to this area.

C.   Whenever it rains, the roof _____ [*leak*; factual] badly.

D.   When we heard the whistle, we _____ [*start*; factual] running toward the

   finish line.

E.   If you purchase this warranty, your money _____ [*refund*; predictive] if the

   product is defective.

1.   Unless we leave now, we _____ not _____ [*get*;

   predictive] to our destination before dark.

2.   If I had known how difficult calculus was, I _____ not

   _____ [*take*; speculative] this course.

3.   Whenever Susie watches a sad movie, she _____ [*cry*; factual].

4.   If you learn to ski at a young age, you _____ not

   _____ [*develop*; predictive] a fear of heights.

5.   If we had been told about the Indian restaurant's wonderful buffet, we

   _____ [*eat*; speculative] there.

35.5   DIRECT AND INDIRECT QUOTATIONS AND QUESTIONS

Directions: Rewrite each of the following direct quotations or questions as an indirect quotation or question, making appropriate changes in subjects and in verb forms.

Example:

Original sentence (direct quotation): She asked, "Tim, why are you so worried about your car?"

Rewritten as indirect quotation: She asked Tim why he was so worried about his car.

A.   My cousin Betty asked, "Do you remember the summer we spent on Martha's Vineyard?"

B.   "Don't come unprepared for the exam," the teacher warned the students.

C.   Bruce asked, "Where do the whales go in the winter?"

D.   "Why did you sit in traffic instead of taking the back roads home?" Uncle Samuel asked when we

arrived two hours late.

E.   "Is this your idea of a good time?" the police officer angrily asked the children defacing the traffic

signs.

1.   During the inquiry he kept repeating, "I didn't see a thing."

2.   As she stepped out of her car at the airport terminal, Linda told her boyfriend, "Please don't bother.

I can handle my bags myself."

3.   Miranda asked, "Do you want to taste the brownies?" I said, "Yes, of course I want to taste them."

4.   "Plant the petunias in a shady corner of the flowerbed," the woman at the garden shop told us.

5.   "Are we going to the zoo or to the aquarium first?" the little girl asked her father.

36.1 USING IDIOMS—SET 1

Directions: In each of the following sentences, underline the idiom used and explain what it means.

Example: Diane didn't come to our party because she was <u>feeling under the weather.</u>

Meaning of idiom: *feeling sick*

A.   Derek announced that he had read a 600-page novel last night, but I took this information with a grain of salt.

B.   The camp counselor told jokes to break the ice at the orientation meeting.

C.   Jeannie was floating on air after Marco asked her for a date.

D.   Olivia gave me the cold shoulder because I hadn't voted for her for class treasurer.

E.   Mrs. Morin gave me the benefit of the doubt when I said that I couldn't finish my essay last night because my printer had run out of ink.

1.   When Jong saw Katrina with her new boyfriend, he blew his top.

2.   Joy said that she needed to borrow the rent money so that she wouldn't be evicted, but her father said that she had cried wolf too many times.

3.   Because Kelly was new at her job, it would take some time before she could learn the ropes.

4.   Darlene put her foot in her mouth when she told Celia that the color of her living room looked like overcooked egg yolks.

5.   I had been on pins and needles until I received my college acceptance letter.

36.2   USING IDIOMS—SET 2

Directions: In each of the following sentences, underline the idiom used and explain what it means.

Example: Jon said that he <u>had a bone to pick</u> with me after he received my complaint letter about his repair job.

Meaning of idiom: *had a problem to settle*

A.   Dad warned us not to go overboard when buying refreshments for the party.

B.   My adviser said I should put my best foot forward at the job interview.

C.   Alonzo kept beating around the bush before finally admitting that he had lost my car keys at the

beach.

D.   Don't rock the boat when the issue comes up for a vote.

E.   I had a rude awakening when I opened my paycheck.

1.   The newest player on the team is really a bad apple.

2.   I'll really have to burn the midnight oil to finish my term paper by tomorrow.

3.   Finding out how much used motor oil ends up in storm drains gave us food for thought.

4.   My mother and I certainly don't see eye to eye about hairstyles.

5.   We learned by word of mouth about the documentary that was critical of Wal-Mart's practices.

12.1 IDENTIFYING TOPIC, RESTRICTING, AND SUPPORTING SENTENCES

A.   _T_ The best-known . . . sixteenth century. _R_ History shows . . . Suleyman.
_S_ A Venetian envoy . . . very gentle." _S_ He wrote poetry . . . he married. _S_ In one poem
. . . my pavilion." _S_ Often called . . . legal procedures. _S_ His code . . . against criminals.

Stanley Meisler, "Splendors of Topkapi," *Smithsonian*,
February 2000: 121.

B.   _T_ Professional boxing . . . to tolerate. _S_ In the ring, . . . swollen eyes. _S_ Mike Tyson . . .
opponent's ear. _S_ Ray "Boom . . . his opponent. _R_ But the damage . . . in the ring. _S_
Sugar Ray . . . the right eye. _S_ Muhammad Ali . . . to the head.

12.2 STAYING ON THE TOPIC

A.   (2) The canyon . . . northern Arizona.
     (8) Later . . . El Tovar.
B.   (5) Other countries . . . similar data.
C.   (4) As their . . . of speed.
D.   (5) Archaeology . . . nineteenth century.
     (7) The human . . . no limits.
E.   (2) Actually, developing . . . them.
     (5) Used enlargers . . . to find.

12.3 ARRANGING YOUR DETAILS (ORGANIZATIONAL STRATEGIES)

A.   Chronological order
B.   Illustration
C.   Analogy
D.   Process
E.   Comparison/contrast

12.4   USING TRANSITIONS AND REPETITION

A.   The custom of the birthday cake began during the thirteenth century in Germany, part of a <u>day-long</u> celebration called *Kinderfest*—or "child festival"—marking the birthday of a child. *Kinderfest* began <u>at dawn</u> when a child was awakened by the arrival of a cake topped with <u>lighted candles</u>. The one <u>candle</u> more than the total of the child's years represented the "<u>light</u> of life." The <u>candles</u> were <u>burned</u> and replaced <u>all day</u> until the cake was eaten <u>after dinner</u>. At this time the child made a wish and blew out the <u>candles</u>. The <u>candles</u> had to be <u>extinguished</u> with a single breath. For the wish to come true, it had to remain a secret.

> Adapted from Charles Panati, *Extraordinary Origins*
> *of Everyday Things* (New York: Harper, 1987), 33.

12.5   PARAGRAPH DIVISION

A.   American mythology makes common cause with another formidable force: American complacency. Harold Stevenson's work in 1979–80 with children, mothers, and teachers from three countries suggests that problem by contrasting performance and attitudes. In one statistical he rated the mathematics achievement of equal numbers of students from Japan, Taiwan, and the United States. Among the top 100 first-graders there were only fifteen American children. Almost unbelievably, among the top 100 fifth-graders there was only one American child. In contrast, among the bottom 100 first-graders, fifty-eight were American, and among the bottom 100 fifth-graders, sixty-seven were American.

There was more. The shocker came in the attitude surveys. More than 40 percent of the American mothers were "very satisfied" with how their children were doing in school, whereas less than 5 percent of the Japanese and Chinese mothers were "very satisfied." Nearly a third of the Chinese and Japanese mothers said they were "not satisfied" with their children's performance, but only 10 percent of the American mothers expressed dissatisfaction.

The jarring enthusiasm of the Americans persisted when it came to attitudes toward the quality of the schools themselves. Ninety-one percent judged that the school was doing an "excellent" or "good" job. Only 42 percent of the Chinese mothers and 39 percent of the Japanese mothers were this positive.

> Michael J. Barrett, "The Case for More School
> Days," *The Atlantic*, November 1990: 94.

13.1   COMBINING SENTENCES—SET 1

Possible revisions:

A.   Rupert hasn't turned in a single paper or piece of homework this semester.

B.   Death Valley, the lowest place in the United States, is also the hottest.

C.   Many television stations in the United States are on the air twenty-four hours a day; however, in many foreign countries the number of broadcasting hours is carefully regulated.

D.   Although they have been separated for two years, Robert and Annie have recently been meeting to try to reconcile.

E.   Knowing how much they enjoyed political humor, we recommended the latest exhibit at the Cartoon Art Museum to our cousins.

13.2   COMBINING SENTENCES—SET 2

Possible revision:

A.   Two literary works, written over a century apart, captured the hysteria of the Salem witch hunts. Nathaniel Hawthorne, whose great-great-grandfather Colonel John Hathorne had been one of the magistrates who had tried those accused of witchcraft, wrote the story "Young Goodman Brown" in 1835. Arthur Miller wrote the play *The Crucible* in 1953. Hawthorne and Miller set their works in 1692 Salem and used as characters some of the real people who had been afflicted and accused. However, Miller wrote his play at the time of another witch hunt, this one directed against alleged Communists in the U.S. government and in the arts and entertainment worlds. Although no one was hanged in the 1950s, many lives were destroyed, and many careers were ended prematurely.

13.3   EXPANDING SENTENCES

Possible answers (expanded parts of sentences are in italics):

A.   Mr. Stevenson planted bamboo in the front yard *to stop his nosy neighbors from looking in his windows.*
infinitive phrase

B.   Bruce *reluctantly* mailed his *huge* mortgage payment.
individual modifiers

C.   *Covered in mud,* Sam emerged from the swimming hole.
participial phrase

D.   *As the dinner was burning on the stove top,* Juanita was busy talking on the phone.
subordinate clause

E.   *Looking exhausted,* Doris declared that she'd had a hard day at work.
participial phrase

13.4   USING ACTIVE AND PASSIVE VOICE

A.   The audience gave the cellist a standing ovation when she finished her solo.

B.   Diligent recyclers have diverted many recyclables from the waste stream.

C.   Sled dogs carrying medical supplies to snowed-in Alaskan villages endure many harsh conditions.

D.   Modern psychoanalysts have disputed Freud's identification of the ego, the id, and the superego as the components of personality.

E.   The lab technicians have tested the blood samples for their DNA content.

13.5   USING STRONG, EFFECTIVE CONSTRUCTIONS

Possible answers:

A.   You need to put the trash out early on Monday mornings.

B.   Our physics instructor always let us turn in our work late if we had a good reason for doing so.

C.   Strong evidence suggests that people are affected by second-hand smoke.

D.   The sales representative demonstrated how the new printer could produce high-quality photographs.

E.   The neighborhood watch group voted to ask the city to assign more police patrols to this area after midnight.

13.6   USING PARALLEL STRUCTURE

A.   Americans invented jazz and developed rock and roll.

B.   Soft contact lenses must be washed daily, cleaned with a special solution, and stored carefully.

C.   To be comfortable at the campsite, they wanted not only to be able to light a decent fire but also to have access to an electrical hookup.

D.   Listening to the birds chirping in the country is better than being bombarded by traffic noise in the city.

E.   Denise enjoys running, knitting, and collecting stuffed animals.

13.7   DIVIDING RAMBLING SENTENCES

Possible revisions:

A.   Discovered in the eighteenth century, sunspots remained a mystery for two centuries, but now scientists are beginning to understand these solar phenomena.

B.   Although millions of American teenagers take the SAT today, this test was not developed until 1926 and was not widely used until 1943.

C.   Although much of the popularity of video games is due to increasingly more sophisticated graphics, the hand-held Game Boy is still the best-selling video game in history.

D. After intriguing generations of scientists, the channel-like features on Mars have recently helped stimulate a search for water on the red planet.

E. As water cascaded over the falls, we watched the salmon leaping into the air and wondered what compelled them to such struggle.

13.8 VARYING SENTENCE STRUCTURE

Possible revisions:

A. When wind speeds exceed seventy-five miles per hour, a tropical storm is called a hurricane.

B. Even though they are now a staple of southern cuisine, grits did not become common in the South until after the Civil War.

C. Although some people still associate animation with children, many cartoons today are designed for adult viewers.

D. Largely because of its author's popularity, Charles Dickens's *A Christmas Carol* sold more than six thousand copies.

E. Machines cannot duplicate the various and highly complex functions of one irreplaceable organ, the liver.

14.1 SELECTING EXACT WORDS

Possible revisions:

A. *Blow-Up* is definitely Antonioni's masterpiece.

B. Most of the money from the fundraiser went to the needy poor.

C. Lack of rainfall and very high temperatures are threatening the corn crop.

D. Honest lawyers who charge fair rates are difficult to find.

E. San Francisco, a city that has twice rebuilt after suffering the devastating effects of two earthquakes, demonstrates that adversity can be overcome with determination.

14.2 CUTTING WORDINESS

Possible revisions:

A. Most magazine advertisements attract the reader's attention with bold designs and bright colors.

B. Combine nutmeg, cinnamon, salt, and flour and then stir the mixture for five minutes.

C. An ovenbird is an American warbler that builds a nest resembling an oven on the forest floor.

D. We watched anxiously as the climbers descended into the ravine; soon they were no longer visible.

E. Many cities have started recycling programs because their landfills have reached capacity.

14.3   EDITING PHRASES AND CLAUSES

Possible revisions:

A.   Mediterranean cuisine features a variety of foods from southern Europe and the Islamic world.
B.   Since the 1930s writers have been attracted to Hollywood as a setting for their novels.
C.   Research assistants help professors at major universities conduct research projects.
D.   Many people consider Simón Bolívar hero because he helped defeat Spanish armies in South America.
E.   Old-growth forests are at least two hundred years old and have never been cut.

14.4   DEVELOPING AN ACADEMIC STYLE

Possible revisions:

A.   I agree with your assessment that the president has too much power.
B.   Ernest bought Honda's new car-based sports utility vehicle that had the optional premium features: power steering, dual suspension, and anti-lock brakes.
C.   When people are young, they do not always recognize their own limitations.
D.   Sometimes American farmers cannot sell their genetically modified crops because European markets will not purchase them.
E.   The new patient in the Intensive Care Unit sustained internal injuries as well as bruises and scraped skin when he fell from a second-story window.

14.5   USING FAIR, RESPECTFUL LANGUAGE

Possible revisions:

A.   Off-duty police officers sometimes encounter crimes in progress.
B.   Maurice has been using a wheelchair since his diving accident.
C.   My mother was a typical suburban homemaker before she started law school.
D.   The nation's founders created the Declaration of Independence and the Bill of Rights to define the rights of American citizens.
E.   Senator Mona Morrison and Representative Tom Robinson addressed the rally.

15.1   USING THE CORRECT WORD—SET 1

A.   well
B.   stationary
C.   supposed to

D.   that
E.   try to

15.2   Using the Correct Word—Set 2

A.   illusion
B.   capital
C.   censured
D.   complemented
E.   eminent

19.1   Identifying Nouns

A.   Some <u>critics</u> believe that <u>people</u> who watch too much <u>television</u> have short attention <u>spans</u>.
B.   A general <u>encyclopedia</u> is a <u>collection</u> of <u>knowledge</u> and <u>information</u> on a broad <u>range</u> of <u>topics</u>.
C.   Early in the twentieth <u>century</u>, two hundred button <u>factories</u> in the <u>United States</u> almost depleted the <u>supply</u> of freshwater <u>mussels</u>.
D.   In <u>1988</u>, <u>divers</u> off the <u>coast</u> of <u>Turkey</u> found <u>jars</u> of baked <u>clay</u> dating from the thirteenth <u>century</u> B.C.
E.   <u>Hikers</u> in <u>Yellowstone National Park</u> are advised to wear <u>layers</u> of <u>clothing</u> and to carry a good <u>supply</u> of <u>water</u>.

19.2   Identifying Pronouns and Antecedents

A.   <u>Nobody</u> spoke against the proposal , but <u>each</u> of <u>us</u> had reasons to object to <u>it</u>.

B.   The football players congratulated <u>themselves</u> for playing a great game and waved to

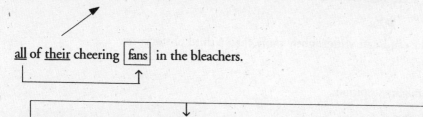

<u>all</u> of <u>their</u> cheering fans in the bleachers.

C.   <u>Most</u> of the nation's small businesses are quite concerned about the rising costs of <u>their</u> employees' health insurance.

D.   <u>These</u> are the ⟦files⟧ that <u>you</u> should return to <u>their</u> original locations.

E.   ⟦People⟧ <u>who</u> live in <u>that</u> part of the country are used to <u>those</u> extreme temperatures.

19.3   FORMS OF PERSONAL PRONOUNS

A.   I
B.   his or her
C.   I
D.   whom
E.   he

19.4   USING RELATIVE PRONOUNS IN RELATIVE AND NOUN CLAUSES

A.   *Whomever*—direct object of the verb *help* in the noun dependent clause, which is the subject of the sentence.

B.   *whoever*—subject of the noun dependent clause, which is the object of the preposition *with*.

C.   *who*—subject of the adjective/relative clause, which modifies *boy*.

D.   *whom*—direct object of the verb *trusted* in the adjective/relative clause, which modifies *person*.

E.   *who*—subject of the adjective/relative clause, which modifies *explorers*.

20.1   CLASSES OF VERBS

$\qquad$ *S   AV AV   DO*
A.   Mary <u>was writing</u> her term paper all night.

$\qquad$ *S   AV*
B.   Some of the voters <u>wondered</u> about the election results.

$\qquad$ *S   LV   PN*
C.   The winner <u>was</u> the candidate with slightly more than a third of the votes.

$\qquad$ *S   AV*
D.   His alibi <u>sounded</u> mighty suspicious.

$\qquad$ *S AV AV   DO*
E.   I <u>have owned</u> this Honda for seventeen years.

20.2 FORMS OF VERBS

A. begun
B. fought
C. darkened
D. froze
E. have watched

20.3 SEQUENCE OF VERB TENSES—SET 1

A. Change *plays* to *played*.
B. Change *was talking* to *has been talking*.
C. Correct
D. Change *climbed* to *have climbed*; change *fell* to *had fallen*.
E. Change *contained* to *contains*.

20.4 SEQUENCE OF VERB TENSES—SET 2

A. Change *destroyed* to *had destroyed*.
B. Change *will be replacing* to *will replace* or *can replace*.
C. Change *were known* to *are known*.
D. Change *revealed* to *reveals*.
E. Correct

20.5 ACTIVE AND PASSIVE VOICE

A. Security officials at airports view unattended luggage very suspiciously.
B. Correct
C. When a German ship torpedoed the *Lusitania,* a British steamer, on May 7, 1915, more than one thousand people lost their lives.
D. The defense attorney asked potential jurors to state their opinions on the death penalty.
E. Television contestants who obtain large cash prizes must pay taxes on their winnings.

20.6 MOOD OF A VERB

A. Change *brought* to *bring*.
B. Correct
C. Change *will* to *would*.

D. Change *went* to *had gone*.

E. Delete *should*.

20.7   IRREGULAR VERBS

A. lay

B. hung

C. dragged

D. set

E. raised

20.8   VERBALS

A. Change *depressed* to *depressing* (present participle—predicate adjective)

B. Change *to study* to *studying* (gerund—direct object)

C. Change *to eat* to *eating* (gerund—direct object)

D. Change *surprising* to *surprised* (past participle—adjective)

E. Change *to make* to *making* (gerund—direct object)

21.1   IDENTIFYING ADJECTIVES (PROPER, PREDICATE)

A.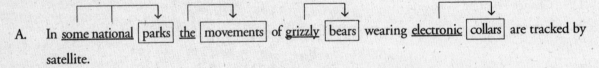
In some national parks the movements of grizzly bears wearing electronic collars are tracked by satellite.

B.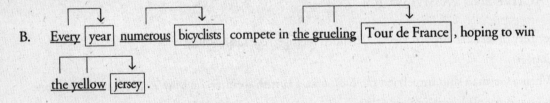
Every year numerous bicyclists compete in the grueling Tour de France, hoping to win the yellow jersey.

C.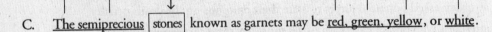
The semiprecious stones known as garnets may be red, green, yellow, or white.

D.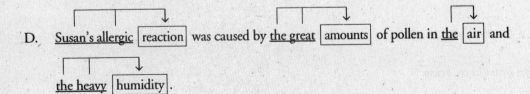
Susan's allergic reaction was caused by the great amounts of pollen in the air and the heavy humidity.

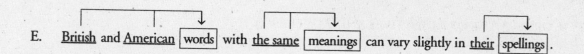

E. British and American words with the same meanings can vary slightly in their spellings.

21.2 IDENTIFYING ADVERBS AND THE ROLES THEY PLAY

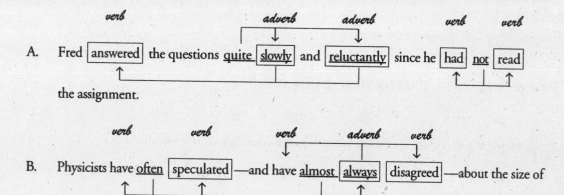

A. Fred answered the questions quite slowly and reluctantly since he had not read the assignment.

B. Physicists have often speculated —and have almost always disagreed —about the size of the universe.

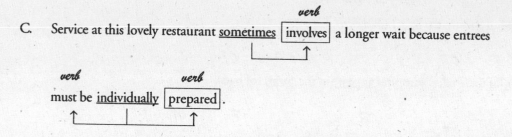

C. Service at this lovely restaurant sometimes involves a longer wait because entrees must be individually prepared.

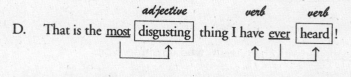

D. That is the most disgusting thing I have ever heard!

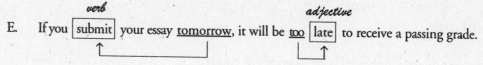

E. If you submit your essay tomorrow, it will be too late to receive a passing grade.

21.3 FORMS OF ADJECTIVES AND ADVERBS

A. coolly
B. bad, worse
C. more slowly
D. most
E. reasonably

21.4 CORRECT USE OF ADJECTIVES AND ADVERBS

A. Change *badly* to *bad*.
B. Delete *very*.
C. Change *real* to *really*.
D. Correct
E. Change *sickly* to *sick*; change *quick* to *quickly*.

21.5 PREPOSITIONS AND PREPOSITIONAL PHRASES

A. Legends (about vampires) are found (in many cultures) (throughout the world).

B. (In most legends) vampires leave their graves (at night) and return (to them) (after a few drinks) (of blood) but (before the light) (of dawn).

C. (In some) (of these tales) vampires appear (in the form) (of bats).

D. Many films (about frightening vampires) have been made (in recent years).

E. (In *Nosferatu*) the title character is a vampire (with sharp teeth) who resembles a rat.

21.6 CONJUNCTIONS

A. *and* Coordinating conjunction connects two independent clauses.
B. *Either . . . or* Correlative conjunctions connect two subjects (compound subject)
C. *or* Coordinating conjunction connects the second and third of three nouns in a series that are objects of the preposition *from*.
D. *because* Subordinating conjunction introduces adverb dependent clause that modifies verb *are*.
E. *but* Coordinating conjunction connects two adverbs.

21.8   REVIEW EXERCISE 2: IDENTIFYING PARTS OF SPEECH

Words in italics are identified as particular parts of speech in the parentheses.

one (pronoun), *most* (adverb), *slowly* (adverb), *near* (preposition), *during* (preposition), *century* (noun), *it* (pronoun), *sea* (adjective), *another* (adjective), *by* (preposition), *If* (subordinating conjunction), *that* (pronoun), *will inundate* (active verb), *Have alarmed* (active verb), *these* (adjective), *Yes!* (interjection), *recently* (adverb), *and* (coordinating conjunction), *more* (pronoun)

22.1   IDENTIFYING SIMPLE AND COMPLETE SUBJECTS

A.   <u>Scorpions, rattlesnakes, gila monsters, and black widow spiders</u> inhabit the deserts of Arizona.

B.   <u>A day at the beach</u> is always relaxing.

C.   <u>Sunken Spanish treasure ships laden with gold, silver, and gems</u> are still being discovered in the Caribbean.

D.   <u>(You)</u> Bring me some dinner right now!

E.   <u>Moving to a new city</u> can be stressful.

22.2   IDENTIFYING PREDICATES

A.   Where <u>did</u> <u>you</u> <u>put the adding machine?</u>

B.   At air shows <u>stunt pilots</u> <u>put their planes into steep power stalls and then slip into dives</u>.

C.   There <u>is</u> <u>no film</u> in a digital camera.

D.   In 1856, <u>Gail Borden</u> <u>discovered a way to keep milk from spoiling and soon became rich</u>.

                         SS   P   P   P   P
E.   At last night's concert <u>people</u> <u>were standing in the aisles, jumping up and down, and cheering</u>
     <u>wildly for the band to continue playing.</u>

22.3   IDENTIFYING COMPLEMENTS AND OTHER SENTENCE ELEMENTS—SET 1

            S   AV   DO
A.   Cemeteries in New Orleans contain many above-ground tombs.

        S   AV IO   DO
B.   Marlene gave Tom her car keys yesterday.

        S   S   LV   PN
C.   Similes and metaphors are common figures of speech.

          S   AV AV   DO OC
D.   The Smiths are painting their new house purple.

          S   LV   PN
E.   Drip irrigation is a very efficient method for watering a garden.

22.4   IDENTIFYING COMPLEMENTS AND OTHER SENTENCE ELEMENTS—SET 2

        S   AV AV IO   DO
A.   The statues found in the tombs of ancient Egypt have brought us many surprises.

        S   AV DO
B.   The Egyptians carved some of the statues from anorthosite gneiss.

      S   LV   PA
C.   These appear deep blue in the sunlight.

        S   LV PA   AV   DO   DO
D.   Other statues are huge and commemorate the power and accomplishments of the pharaohs.

        S   AV   DO
E.   The Egyptians considered the tombs' life-sized statues, astonishingly realistic and beautifully

            OC
     painted, repositories of the *ka*, or soul, of the dead.*

* Adapted from Bennett Schiff, "Out of Egypt: Art in the Age of the Pyramids," *Smithsonian* 30.6
(1999): 108–119.

22.5   IDENTIFYING FRAGMENTS

A.   S
     F
B.   F
     F
C.   F
     S
D.   F
     F
E.   F
     S

22.6   TYPES OF SENTENCES: IDENTIFYING INDEPENDENT AND DEPENDENT CLAUSES— SET 1

A.   Some adventurers use ice axes, spiked boots, and crampons to scale frozen waterfalls, but their success really depends on skill, stamina, and steady nerves.
     compound

B.   On October 12, 1999, the world's population reached six billion, according to the United Nations Fund for Population Activities.
     simple

C.   Hybrid bicycles, which can be very expensive, are a cross between mountain bicycles and racers; some cyclists refer to them as cross-terrain models.
     compound-complex

D.   Because they had studied all semester, the students performed well on the physics exam.
     complex

E.   Moving south through Vermont, New Hampshire, Massachusetts, and Connecticut, the Connecticut River eventually reaches the Atlantic Ocean.
     simple

22.7   TYPES OF SENTENCES: IDENTIFYING INDEPENDENT AND DEPENDENT CLAUSES— SET 2

A.   Poland's Wielicaka salt mine, which has been in use since the thirteenth century, contains many beautiful sculptures carved from salt by generations of miners.
     complex

B.   The search party has been looking all day for the hikers, but they seem to have vanished without leaving a trace.

compound

C.   Large amounts of fresh water pouring into the ocean from flooded rivers can hurt some kinds of sea life, especially shellfish.

simple

D.   Many people believe that King Arthur, the ruler of Camelot, was a real person, but no conclusive proof of his existence has ever been found.

compound-complex

E.   (You) Look under your chair if you are really brave.

complex

22.8   KINDS OF SENTENCES

A.   Interrogative
B.   Declarative
C.   Imperative
D.   Exclamatory
E.   Declarative

23.1   PREPOSITIONAL PHRASES

```
             adjective                    adverb          adverb
        P          OP              P        OP      P      OP
```
A.   The family (of Mexican immigrants) drove (across the country) (in five days).

```
       adverb       adjective                                    adverb
      P    OP       P     OP                              P         OP
```
B.   (In the middle) (of the night) our fears seem much greater than they do (during the daytime).

```
         adjective              adverb            adverb
        P  OP               P    OP      P            OP
```
C.   The swarm (of locusts) appeared (in our area) (during the early summer) and really annoyed us
```
          adverb
       P      OP
```
     (with their noise).

adjective

P   OP

D.   Wetlands provide ecological bases (for wildlife); however, they are quite vulnerable

adverb   *adjective*   *adverb*

P   OP   P OP   P   OP

(to development), which has destroyed most (of them) (in the continental United States).

adjective   *adverb*

P OP   OP   OP   P   OP

E.   A crown (of rubies, emeralds, and diamonds) worn (by many ancient British kings) is now

adverb   *adverb*   *adjective*

P   OP   P   OP   P   OP

(on display) (in the Tower) (of London's) jewelry museum.

23.2   VERBAL PHRASES—SET 1

A.   Many war-game enthusiasts re-create battles of the past by <u>using miniature soldiers and carefully</u>
<u>reconstructed battlefields</u>.
gerund phrase with two objects of gerund—acts as object of preposition <u>by</u>

B.   The scientists, <u>concerned about the potential health hazards</u>, made their most recent research
findings public.
participial phrase—acts as adjective modifying <u>scientists</u>

C.   <u>Stretching for several blocks</u>, the traffic jam tested the commuters' patience.
participial phrase—acts as adjective modifying <u>traffic jam</u>

D.   <u>To visit the Baseball Hall of Fame</u> is the dream of many young boys.
infinitive phrase used as a noun—subject of sentence

E.   <u>Swimming two or three times a week</u> can keep a person in good health.
gerund phrase—subject of sentence

23.3   VERBAL PHRASES—SET 2

A.   <u>Dying at a rate of about one species every 1,000 years</u>, dinosaurs during the "great dying" actually
took 50 to 75 million years to become extinct.
participial phrase—adjective modifying <u>dinosaurs</u>

B.   Jack's plan <u>to find the buried treasure</u> was really a futile daydream.
infinitive phrase—adjective modifying <u>plan</u>

C.   We were quite eager <u>to reach our destination</u>.
     infinitive phrase—adverb modifying predicate adjective <u>eager</u>

D.   <u>Finishing the last chapter of her novel</u> was much more difficult than the author had anticipated.
     gerund phrase—subject of sentence

E.   Brazil, <u>motivated by the need for an additional energy source</u>, has produced gasohol from sugar as a viable alternative to gasoline.
     participial phrase—adjective modifying <u>Brazil</u>

23.4   IDENTIFYING OTHER PHRASES AND THEIR FUNCTIONS

A.   absolute phrase—modifies whole independent clause
B.   prepositional phrase—acts as adverb that answers the question "When?"
C.   appositive phrase—renames subject
D.   two prepositional phrases—one adverb (answers question "When?") and one adjective (modifies *end*)
E.   verb phrase—main verb of sentence

24.1   IDENTIFYING INDEPENDENT AND DEPENDENT CLAUSES—SET 1

A.   <u>Ice cream, which was commercially made as early as 1786, was first sold in New York.</u>
     adjective dependent clause—modifies <u>ice cream</u>
B.   <u>Whoever opens the door</u> will be surprised by our Halloween costumes.
     noun dependent clause—subject of sentence
C.   Anyone <u>who decides to run for president</u> must file a financial statement with the Federal Election Commission.
     adjective dependent clause—modifies <u>Anyone</u>
D.   Jacques Cousteau invented the aqualung |while| <u>he was a member of the French Underground during World War II.</u>
     adverb dependent clause—modifies verb <u>invented</u> (answers question "When?")
E.   <u>Hawaii is the only one of the United States</u> <u>that produces coffee.</u>
     adjective dependent clause—modifies <u>one</u>

24.2   IDENTIFYING INDEPENDENT AND DEPENDENT CLAUSES—SET 2

A. |While| <u>Samuel Johnson was compiling his famous dictionary,</u> he employed the services of four <u>assistants.</u>
     adverb dependent clause—modifies verb <u>employed</u>
B.   <u>How Nigel keeps that car running</u> is a mystery to us.
     noun dependent clause—subject of sentence

C. <u>Rasheed accepted an offer to play professional basketball in Poland</u> $\boxed{\text{although}}$ <u>he would have preferred to stay in the United States</u>.
adverb dependent clause—modifies verb <u>*accepted*</u>

D. <u>Mrs. Tyler advertised for a housekeeper</u> <u>who would shop for groceries, prepare meals, and do laundry</u>.
adjective dependent clause—modifies <u>*housekeeper*</u>

E. <u>The Internet has profoundly changed the ways</u> <u>that stocks are bought and sold</u>.
adjective dependent clause—modifies <u>*ways*</u>

24.3 IDENTIFYING NOUN CLAUSES AND THEIR FUNCTIONS

A. Some people once believed <u>that the world was flat</u>.
direct object

B. <u>How Houdini performed many of his amazing feats</u> remains a mystery to this day.
subject

C. Ted will give the jackpot to <u>whoever shows up with the winning ticket</u>.
object of preposition <u>*to*</u>

D. We realized <u>(that) Harold's daughters only come to visit on alternate Fridays</u>.
direct object

E. Knowing <u>what was expected of them</u> enabled the gymnasts to perform their routines effortlessly.
object of gerund <u>*Knowing*</u>

24.4 IDENTIFYING ADJECTIVE CLAUSES AND THEIR FUNCTIONS

A. The city council's parking permit proposal, <u>which was too long and needlessly complex,</u> was nevertheless adopted by a majority vote.
modifies <u>*proposal*</u>

B. AmTrak has added three more trains <u>that will travel directly between Boston and New York</u>.
modifies <u>*trains*</u>

C. The interns <u>who were hired last summer</u> will be staying on full time.
modifies <u>*interns*</u>

D. The answers <u>that you gave</u> didn't make sense.
modifies <u>*answers*</u>

E. Horace, <u>whom you had recommended for the job</u>, did not impress the interviewer.
modifies <u>*Horace*</u>

24.5   IDENTIFYING RESTRICTIVE AND NONRESTRICTIVE CLAUSES—SET 1

A.   *R R*   Runners who stretch before they run have fewer injuries than those who don't stretch.

B.   *N-R*   Nylon, which can be woven into delicate lingerie, can also be incorporated into durable machinery parts.   *commas added*

C.   *R*   The potato is one of the major food crops that originated in America.

D.   *R*   The lawyer whom I hired is a specialist in work accident litigation.

E.   *N-R*   Air bags, which were once considered impractical luxury features, are now standard equipment on most vehicles.   *commas added*

24.6   IDENTIFYING RESTRICTIVE AND NONRESTRICTIVE CLAUSES—SET 2

A.   *N-R*   Robotic surgery, which is still considered experimental, has the highest success rate in the treatment of prostate cancer.   *commas added*

B.   *R*   The man who sat next to me on the subway picked my pocket.

C.   *N-R*   To understand the British system of nobility, which is usually referred to as *the peerage*, one needs to know something about British history.   *commas added*

D.   *R R*   The proposal that got the most votes was not the one that we supported.

E.   *R*   The hours of the after-school day-care program are meant to accommodate children whose parents work evenings.

24.7   IDENTIFYING ADVERB CLAUSES AND THEIR FUNCTIONS

A.   Artists have favored oil paint for hundreds of years | because | it dries slowly and does not crack.
modifies verb have favored

B.   After the hurricane the waves were larger | than | any we had ever seen before.
modifies adjective larger

C.   Bob and Karen were running | as | quickly | as | they could move to catch the train pulling out of the station.
modifies adverb quickly

D. | Although | the word *hound* once referred to any kind of dog, it is now mainly used to indicate certain kinds of hunting dogs.
modifies verb is used

E. | When | it's noon in Boston in the summer, it's 6 a.m. in Hawaii.
modifies verb is (in contraction it's)

25.1   SUBJECT–VERB AGREEMENT: PERSON AND NUMBER, DELAYED SUBJECTS

	Simple Subject	Correct Verb
A.	One	needs
B.	coach	leads
C.	tip	lies
D.	box	is
E.	singer	is

25.2   SUBJECT–VERB AGREEMENT: COMPOUND SUBJECTS, COLLECTIVE NOUNS

	Simple Subject(s)	Correct Verb
A.	buyers, seller	knows
B.	teacher, adviser	is
C.	news	was
D.	Pork and beans	is
E.	faculty	are

25.3   SUBJECT–VERB AGREEMENT: NUMBERS AND NUMERICAL TERMS AS SUBJECTS

	Simple Subject	Correct Verb
A.	percentage	were
B.	number	is
C.	bushes	were
D.	number	are
E.	hours	was

25.4   SUBJECT–VERB AGREEMENT: RELATIVE AND INDEFINITE PRONOUNS AS SUBJECTS

	Simple Subject	Correct Verb
A.	Nobody	has
B.	Most	has
C.	Everything	has
D.	flu	have
E.	Some	have

25.5   OTHER SUBJECT–PREDICATE ERRORS

	Simple Subject(s)	Correct Verb
A.	special	is
B.	*The Martian Chronicles*	is
C.	interest	was
D.	*Organic ingredients*	is
E.	paintings	are

25.6   PRONOUN–ANTECEDENT AGREEMENT—SET 1

	Antecedent(s)	Correct Pronoun(s)
A.	children, Mrs. Greene	her
B.	Everything	its
C.	horse	that
D.	No one	his or her
E.	crew	its

25.7   PRONOUN–ANTECEDENT AGREEMENT—SET 2

	Incorrect Pronoun(s) (Circled)	Correct Pronoun(s)
A.	it	them
B.	he, his	he or she, his or her
C.	who	that
D.	Correct	
E.	their	his or her

25.8   AMBIGUOUS AND VAGUE ANTECEDENTS

Possible revisions:

A. After returning from his vacation, Jack went to visit David.

B. Brad is a senior citizen, a designation that qualifies him for a discount at the movies.

C. After my flight had been canceled and I had missed my connection, the airline put me up in a hotel and gave me vouchers for cabs and meals.

D. Kevin plays his stereo full blast all night long, and his neighbors don't like the noise.

E. Andrea left part of her car sticking out of the driveway, a careless parking maneuver that caused the car to be hit by a speeding truck.

26.1   CORRECTING SENTENCE FRAGMENTS

A.   *Fragment underlined:* Those being England, Scotland, and Wales.
     Possible revision: The island of Britain actually contains three different countries: England, Scotland, and Wales.

B.   *Fragment underlined:* Such as those that consider men more important than women.
     Possible revision: In some cultures, such as those that consider men more important than women, it is a constant struggle for a woman to gain the respect of men.

C.   *Fragment underlined:* After we tipped the doorman generously.
     Possible revision: We were finally admitted to the exclusive nightclub after we tipped the doorman generously.

D.   *Fragment underlined:* Still visible after centuries of use and neglect.
     Possible revision: Still visible after centuries of use and neglect, Roman roads can be traced in many parts of Europe today.

E.   *Fragment underlined:* And empties into the Potomac.
     Possible revision: Unlike most rivers in North America, the Shenandoah flows north and empties into the Potomac.

26.2   CORRECTING COMMA SPLICES

Possible revisions:

A.   Because he didn't like to waste time sticking in a new sheet, Jack Kerouac used long, continuous rolls of paper while writing on his typewriter.

B.   People who talk on their cell phones while driving are hazards to other drivers.

C.   Some comets orbit the earth every few years; however, others take thousands of years to circle the planet.

D.   Feeling lucky yesterday, Terry bought a lottery ticket.

E.   Medical science has extended life expectancy. Consequently, people need to develop hobbies that can become meaningful activities in retirement.

26.3   CORRECTING FUSED/RUN-ON SENTENCES

Possible revisions:

A.   Because she rarely got to play during soccer practice, Julia didn't expect to score a goal in the game.

B.   Some tides change approximately every twelve hours. The moon is the cause of these massive shifts of ocean water.

C.   Many people enjoy the freedom that comes with working at home; however, they must be disciplined in order to be productive.

D.   I arrived on campus at 8 a.m. this morning, but I still couldn't find a parking space.

E.   High-frequency sound waves have many medical applications, such as determining the health and even the gender of a fetus in the womb.

26.4   REVIEW EXERCISE: CORRECTING FRAGMENTS, COMMA SPLICES, AND RUN-ONS

Possible revision:

A.   Although turquoise was mined by Egyptian pharaohs more than five thousand years ago and traded by Chinese emperors for centuries, most Americans associate this beautiful stone with their own desert southwest. They do so for good reason. More than a thousand years ago, ancient Mayans were importing turquoise from what is now New Mexico. These mines were surprisingly large, and archaeologists estimate that Native American miners dug thousands of tons of rock. However, fewer than twenty active mines are in this country today. Most of the turquoise dug now comes from China.

Adapted from Joseph Harris, "Tantalizing Turquoise,"
Smithsonian 30.5 (1999): 70–80.

26.5   SHIFTS IN SENTENCE CONSTRUCTION—SET 1

Possible revisions:

A.   The Connecticut River, the longest waterway in New England, drains an area of eleven thousand square miles as it flows from the Canadian border to Long Island Sound.

B.   First, job candidates need to fill out an application form; then they should ask for an interview.

C.   The psychology professor told Felix to hand in his paper by 2 p.m. and asked him if he realized that its being three days late would affect his grade.

D.   Anyone planning on climbing Mt. Rainier needs to anticipate all of the hazards that he or she might encounter.

E.   Marcus said we should come over for dinner and bring some dessert.

26.6   SHIFTS IN SENTENCE CONSTRUCTION—SET 2

Possible revisions:

A.   The proposal to tear down city hall was made by the city council, not by the mayor.

B.   Climbing the last thousand feet of Mauna Kea volcano made us dizzy and lightheaded.

C.   A person should always look in all directions before he or she enters a crosswalk.

D.   The landlord said that we should put the key under the mat after viewing the apartment and that we shouldn't disturb the tenants in the building.

E.   People sometimes twist facts about themselves, such as the places where they have worked, to help themselves save face.

26.7   FAULTY PARALLELISM

Possible revisions:

A.   Dragonflies can fly twenty-five miles per hour, take off backwards, and see behind as well as in front of themselves.

B.   Louise was surprised and excited upon learning that she had won the dance competition.

C.   The superstitious English of the sixteenth and seventeenth centuries were afraid of moonless nights and terrified of black cats.

D.   Working on the assembly line was not only physically exhausting but also confusing.

E.   The collapse of her business venture left Rose penniless, ill, and angry.

26.8   MISPLACED AND DANGLING MODIFIERS—SET 1

Possible revisions:

A.   Visitors can journey to a town nestled between two mountains that has remained unchanged for two centuries.

B.   Many political candidates promise to deal with controversial issues openly.

C.   To play tennis well, one needs to practice frequently.

D.   Arriving home after midnight, we found the house dark.

E.   Since breaking my leg, I've had Kent help me with my household chores.

26.9   MISPLACED AND DANGLING MODIFIERS—SET 2

Possible revisions:

A.   As we waited for the elevator, a mouse ran through the crowd.

B.   Correct

C.   Listening to the ten o'clock news, Martina heard that the rapist had been arrested.

D.   Working cautiously, the air traffic controller guided Flight 774 to a safe landing.

E.   While I was visiting friends, my motorcycle was stolen.

26.10 AMBIGUOUS WORDING

Possible revisions:

A.   Tina has always subscribed to *Vogue*, but she might not continue to do so.
B.   Denver is larger than any other city in Colorado.
C.   Manuel enjoys his sports car more than Linda does.
D.   The hothouse tomatoes from the farm stand are as expensive as but tastier than those from the gourmet market.
E.   Sri Lanka, formerly Ceylon, has been and continues to be the world's chief supplier of natural cinnamon.

26.11 NONSTANDARD LANGUAGE

Possible revisions:

A.   You should have let us know that you would be arriving late.
B.   Gillian could scarcely believe her luck when she found out that she had won the big prize.
C.   The deejay played my favorite song from the new Rolling Stones album.
D.   That child was left unattended at the grocery store.
E.   Dorothy said that my clothing is outdated.

27.1 USING PERIODS

A.   Call me in the morning if you don't feel better.
B.   Most states observe daylight-saving time (DST) (Arizona is the only state that doesn't), but some counties within those states do not observe the seasonal time change.
C.   Meet me at 10 a.m. at the town clock.
D.   Correct
E.   It took Phillip ten years to complete his Ph.D.

27.2 USING QUESTION MARKS

A.   Will you—can you—repair my car before the end of the week?
B.   Am I supposed to know the answers to those difficult math problems?
C.   Really, why didn't I think of that?
D.   Mrs. Brown (is that her real name?) claims to be a descendent of Napoleon.
E.   Correct

27.3   USING EXCLAMATION POINTS

A.   "The car is rolling down the hill!" Joe screamed.
B.   "I wish you would arrive on time!" thundered Harold.
C.   Correct
D.   Halt! Who goes there?
E.   "Don't track that mud on my clean rug, or you'll be sorry!" exclaimed Aunt Tillie.

28.1   USING COMMAS WITH COMPOUNDS AND IN COMPOUND SENTENCES

A.   Before going to the Philippines, we tried to teach ourselves Tagalog, but we finally had to admit defeat and find a teacher to help us.
B.   We wanted to eat at the new Thai restaurant, but it was closed for repairs.
C.   People who have purchased advance tickets and people who are Gold Card members may board the airplane first.
D.   I had the flu last week, so I had to miss the New Year's Eve party.
E.   Don't place anything flammable on the space heater or near the halogen lamp.

28.2   USING COMMAS IN A SERIES

A.   Correct
B.   Some colds begin with a runny nose, others begin with chills, and still others begin when a person feels excessively weak and tired.
C.   A number of political parties, including the Federalist Party, the Whig Party, and the Democrat-Republican Party, played important roles in America's past.
D.   Neither rain nor sleet nor snow delays the delivery of the U.S. mail.
E.   Many pioneers brought little more than a rifle, an ax, a plowshare, and a few simple carpentry tools on their journey west.

28.3   USING COMMAS WITH MODIFIERS

A.   Correct
B.   Living near the ocean involves putting up with ever-present long-legged spiders and great numbers of tiny ants.
C.   Modern farmers use systemic cotton defoliants to allow mechanical harvesters easier access to opened bolls.
D.   We picked a particularly cold day to view the ice sculptures in the park.
E.   Radio talk shows attract many outspoken, opinionated callers.

28.4   USING COMMAS WITH INTRODUCTORY WORDS

A.   To learn how to operate the new computer program, you will need to study the manual.
B.   Wearing a beaded collar, the poodle pranced around the ring.
C.   Built in 1769 and used to pull French artillery, the world's first automobile, a steam carriage, was invented by Captain Nicolas Cugnot.
D.   Nevertheless, we decided to leave the party early because we were tired.
E.   Soon after the laser was created in 1960, scientists began searching for ways to use it in medicine.

28.5   USING COMMAS WITH ENDING WORDS

A.   Mrs. Robinson's job involved entering data that had been submitted by FBI agents from around the country.
B.   Correct
C.   The State Department's decoding unit hired the translator who had lived in Iraq for seven years.
D.   The class enjoyed reading this version of the *Aeneid*, which was written in the original Latin.
E.   We were surprised by the early arrival of Uncle Charles, who always shows up extremely late for family gatherings.

28.6   USING COMMAS WITH INTERRUPTING WORDS

A.   Bald eagles, which can be found mainly in wilderness areas, usually prefer a diet of fish.
B.   Frank's wife, Darlene, always knew all the neighborhood gossip first.
C.   Correct
D.   The Parthenon, which was completed in 432 B.C., is the best surviving example of classical Greek architecture.
E.   The grant that Fernando received will provide him with a modest stipend so that he can finish his research.

28.7   USING COMMAS WITH DIALOGUE, INTERJECTIONS, AND TAGS

A.   You, my students, are the first people to read my new story.
B.   Patrick Henry said, "Give me liberty or give me death."
C.   "Why," asked the hairdresser, "did you dye your hair pink?"
D.   The parking lot attendant said that this lot is usually full by 10 a.m.
E.   "Let's leave, Ellen," Brad said to his friend as he opened the door.

28.8 USING COMMAS WITH TITLES, INITIALS, ADDRESSES, AND NUMBERS

A. That quotation can be found on page 1235.

B. Jamie will begin his new job in November 2007.

C. America entered World War II on December 7, 1941, when Japanese planes attacked Pearl Harbor.

D. The commencement speakers were Carolyn Williams, Ph.D., and Robert Wilson, Jr., a local philanthropist.

E. The MacKay family has lived in Arlington, Virginia, for many years but also has roots in York, Maine, and Edina, Illinois.

28.9 USING COMMAS TO PREVENT CONFUSION

A. After all, the packages did finally arrive.

B. The mayor wanted answers, not excuses, from the commission.

C. Before eating, Ralph introduced all of the guests to each other.

D. Those who serve, serve us well.

E. After losing, the team did not feel much like celebrating.

28.10 AVOIDING COMMA ERRORS

A. The ribbed vault, the flying buttress, and the pointed arch are characteristic of Gothic architecture.

B. Sometimes the cost of meals purchased during business trips can be deducted from taxable income.

C. The investigator was surprised to discover that the front door was locked and that an alarm system had been installed.

D. The city hopes that construction of the new hospital will be completed before the college students return in the fall.

E. In the American justice system, a defendant is considered innocent until proven guilty.

28.11 REVIEW EXERCISE: USING COMMAS CORRECTLY—SET 1

A. Samuel Johnson, one of England's most colorful men of letters, lived a life filled with contradictions. He was a scholarly man, fluent in Greek, Latin, and French, but he welcomed many poor, uneducated people into his household. Although a deeply religious man, he frequently suffered from religious doubts. He had a reputation for sloth, yet he almost single-handedly compiled the first comprehensive English dictionary, a remarkable feat when one considers that he was nearly blind as a result of a childhood case of scrofula. Although his contemporaries knew him as a poet, an essayist, and a brilliant conversationalist, he is perhaps best remembered today as a lexicographer.

29.1   USING SEMICOLONS

A.   To unwind after our final exam, we spent the evening watching a marathon of old romantic movies: *The Philadelphia Story*, starring Katharine Hepburn, Cary Grant, and James Stewart; *Roman Holiday*, with Audrey Hepburn and Gregory Peck; and the all-time classic *Casablanca*, with Humphrey Bogart and Ingrid Bergman.

B.   Water shortages are a serious problem in this area; consequently, many restaurants now only serve water when customers specifically request it.

C.   When parents look for good day-care services, they must consider the reputation of the provider; the size, location, and quality of the facilities; and the ratio of staff members to children.

D.   In 1900, the average life expectancy for an American was 47.3 years; by 1975, this average had increased to 72.4 years.

E.   Some specimens of the bristlecone pine are more than 4,000 years old; this extreme age makes them the oldest living things on Earth.

29.2   USING COLONS

A.   For his birthday Martin wanted new running shoes, some video games, and a stopwatch.

B.   Over vacation I read *Hardcore Troubadour: The Life and Near Death of Steve Earle*.

C.   To restore company profits, the consultant recommended three actions: cut employee wages, increase advertising, and eliminate stock options.

D.   Many theaters find that an 8:15 curtain time results in fewer latecomers than one at 8:00.

E.   Two anticipated effects of the storm were increased erosion of the shoreline and a flash flood in the center of town.

29.3   USING HYPHENS

A.   In keeping with the newly established regulations, this facility is now scent free.

B.   Don't try to re-create the entire program; just do the best that you can.

C.   Three-quarters of the way through the exam, I realized that I didn't know enough about post-Reconstruction America to answer the last essay question.

D.   Mother received a beautifully embroidered shawl from her eldest daughter and some scented soaps from her sister-in-law.

E.   Molly had always resented Marlin's devil-may-care attitude.

29.4 USING DASHES

A. This part of the report is important—at least to me—so pay attention.
B. The most common means of evaluation—the intelligence test—is no longer considered sufficient as the sole indicator for determining whether to place students in a special education class.
C. The northern New England states—Maine, New Hampshire, and Vermont—are likely to experience fuel shortages if this is a cold winter.
D. Several of the professors—I can't remember all of their names right now—signed the petition.
E. Some presidents—John F. Kennedy, for example—seem larger than life in the backward glance of historical perspective.

29.5 USING SEMICOLONS, COLONS, AND DASHES

A. We saw a hastily scrawled note on the cabin door that let us know we weren't welcome: NO VISITORS.
B. Victims of Hurricane Katrina can use any basic supplies that you can spare—food, water, clothing, medicine, or blankets. [Colon would also be acceptable.]
C. The thief's plan was obvious: break the window, cut the wires, snatch the jewels, and climb down the fire escape.
D. The project seemed like it would never end; it lasted a week longer than scheduled.
E. The experiment addressed the following effects of sleep deprivation: listlessness, irritability, and the inability to concentrate.

29.6 USING PARENTHESES AND BRACKETS

A. The coded message read, "Tell the boss [Senator Butler] that the eagle [the German ambassador] has landed."
B. Some options for savers (mutual funds, tax-exempt bonds, and zero-coupon bonds) are not understood by many consumers.
C. The term *gross national product (GNP)* refers to the total value of goods and services that a country produces in one year.
D. "I have now reviewed the evidance [*sic*]," said the attorney, "and I believe that I can defend you properly."
E. Descriptions may be *objective* (focusing on the object itself) or *subjective* (focusing on the individual's response to the object).

29.7   USING APOSTROPHES

A.   The mechanic's estimate was lower than those of his competitors, so I took your advice and had him fix my car.

B.   While Joe was waiting in his boss's office, he reviewed Lawrence's and Emily's attendance records.

C.   The children's clothing was soaked from the unexpected downpours.

D.   I received three A's and two B's on my report card, so my grades were higher than anyone else's in the class.

E.   I'll sew the costumes if you'll paint the sets.

29.8   USING QUOTATION MARKS—SET 1

A.   Why were we assigned Doris Lessing's story "The Old Chief Mshlanga"?

B.   Sonya in Chekhov's *Uncle Vanya* says, "When a woman isn't beautiful, people always say, 'You have lovely eyes[;] you have lovely hair.'"

C.   "One small step for [a] man, one giant step for mankind," Neil Armstrong said as he set foot on the moon in July 1969.

D.   The novel's first chapter, "A Tortuous Beginning," was so confusing that I refused to continue reading.

E.   "Look out!" Manuel exclaimed. "That big boulder is headed your way!"

29.9   USING QUOTATION MARKS—SET 2

A.   "I think that I shall never see / a billboard lovely as a tree," wrote Ogden Nash in a parody of Joyce Kilmer's poem "Trees."

B.   When did Howard Stern start referring to himself as the "King of All Media"?

C.   "Who said, 'You can't step in the same river twice'?" asked the philosophy professor.

D.   "Give me different mothers," St. Augustine said, "and I will give you a different world."

E.   Babe Ruth's amazing ability to hit home runs earned him the nickname "Sultan of Swat."

29.10   USING ITALICS

A.   *Lorry* is the British word for *truck*.

B.   The French use the expression *bon appetit* at the beginning of a meal, but many Americans simply say, "Enjoy."

C.   Charles Lindbergh flew solo across the Atlantic in *The Spirit of St. Louis*.

D.   The *wat*, or Buddhist temple, serves as the social and religious center of most Thai villages.

E.   Some people say they have encountered ghosts aboard the ocean liner *Queen Mary*.

29.11 PUNCTUATING TITLES

A.   The first song on *A Mighty Field of Vision*, a CD anthology of the music of recently rediscovered soul singer Eddie Hinton, is "I Got the Feeling."

B.   Tim Robbins starred in *Jacob's Ladder*, a film that deals with a Vietnam veteran's frightening flashbacks.

C.   The film *Finding Neverland* told how J. M. Barrie, played by Johnny Depp, came to write the play *Peter Pan*.

D.   Gabriel García Márquez, a Colombian-born, Nobel Prize–winning novelist, wrote *One Hundred Years of Solitude*.

E.   The poem "Video Cuisine" appears in Maxine Kumin's collection *The Long Approach*.

29.12 USING ELLIPSIS POINTS

A.   Ursula Le Guin believes:

Science fiction is the mythology of the modern world—or one of its mythologies[,] . . . for science fiction does use the mythmaking faculty to apprehend the world we live in, a world profoundly shaped and changed by science and technology; and its originality is that it uses the mythmaking faculty on new material.

> Ursula K. Le Guin, "Myth and Archetype in Science Fiction," in *The Language of the Night: Essays on Fantasy and Science Fiction*, ed. Susan Wood (New York: Berkley Books, 1982), 64.

B.   How do we define *trash*? Susan Strasser maintains that we determine what we consider trash "by sorting. Everything that comes into the end-of-the-millennium home . . . eventually requires a decision: keep it or toss it. We use it up, we save it to use later, we give it away, or at some point we define it as rubbish, to be taken back out, removed beyond the borders of the household."

> *Waste and Want: A Social History of Trash* (New York: Holt, 1999), 5.

C.   Hugh Howard tells us that "determining the vintage of a house is more than a matter of chronology. Establishing the year in which it was constructed is just a starting point . . . in understanding and appreciating a house."

> *How Old Is This House?* (New York: Noonday Press / Farrar, 1989), xiii.

D. Although most people associate epic poems such as Homer's *The Iliad* and *The Odyssey* with the poetry of ancient Greece, there were also shorter poems created "for private occasions, and particularly to entertain guests at the cultivated drinking parties known as *symposia*. . . . These poems were often full of passion, whether love or hatred, and could be personal or, often, highly political."

> *The Greek Islands*, ed. Isabel Carlyle et al. (New York: DK Publishing, 1998), 54.

E. In Stephen Crane's short story "The Blue Hotel," the action develops as one of the hotel guests, the paranoid Swede, loses control of himself as he gets drunk:

At six-o'clock supper, the Swede fizzed like a fire-wheel. He sometimes seemed on the point of bursting into riotous song, and in all his madness he was encouraged by old Scully. . . . The Swede dominated the whole feast, and he gave it the appearance of a crude bacchanal. He seemed to have grown suddenly taller; he gazed, brutally disdainful, into every face. His voice rang through the room.

> Stephen Crane, "The Blue Hotel," in *The Red Badge of Courage and Other Stories*, ed. Richard Chase (Boston: Houghton Mifflin, 1960), 263.

30.1 CAPITALIZING FIRST WORDS

A. When did Mae West say, "Too much of a good thing can be wonderful"?
B. "You can have some dessert," Aunt Lucy told the children, "if you behave yourselves."
C. There's only one explanation for the Enron executives' actions: greed.
D. Correct
E. We will drive you to the train station (first we will have to figure out where it is) and then go grocery shopping.

30.2 CAPITALIZING PROPER NOUNS

A. More than seven hundred years ago, the Anasazi people of the American Southwest built cliff dwellings that continue to amaze visitors today.
B. F. Scott Fitzgerald's story "The Diamond as Big as the Ritz" contains a theme that would reappear in *The Great Gatsby*.
C. Maurice advised us to drive north for several hours before heading east on I-80.
D. I have to take English literature, world history, and Calculus 101 to complete my graduation requirements.
E. The Norman Conquest of England, led by William the Conqueror, began in 1066.

30.3   CAPITALIZING OTHER WORDS

A.   Jamal moved to the South because he could no longer deal with winters in the Northeast.

B.   Barbara would rather post humorous family pictures on her Web site than send them in the U.S. Mail.

C.   Harold Born, senior vice president, has worked for the company for twenty years.

D.   The Republican Party was known as the antislavery party at the time of the Civil War.

E.   Some conservatives consider those who opposed the invasion of Iraq to be un-American.

31.1   SPOTTING MISSPELLED WORDS

Note: Corrected words are underlined.

A.   Louise and I always end up in an <u>argument</u> when we start discussing politics.

B.   Desmond <u>preferred</u> staying home and listening to classical music while his twin brother Brent enjoyed hearing loud rock bands at smoke-<u>filled</u> clubs.

C.   Russell's <u>judgment</u> was <u>impaired</u> when he hadn't had enough sleep.

D.   We <u>really</u> enjoyed visiting the zebras and the <u>monkeys</u> at the San Diego Zoo.

E.   Brad was <u>truly</u> sorry about the <u>dreadful</u> condition of the driveway.

31.2   FORMING PLURALS

Note: Corrected words are underlined.

A.   The two music stores compete to offer the lowest prices for their <u>CDs</u> [or <u>CD's</u>].

B.   The <u>children's</u> parents had packed their <u>lunches</u> before sending them off on the hike.

C.   Henry VIII had two of his six <u>wives</u> executed.

D.   Correct

E.   The doctor told me to put two <u>spoonfuls</u> of honey in my tea and to take my <u>vitamins</u> every morning.

31.3   REVIEW EXERCISE: SPELLING

Note: Corrected words are underlined.

A.   The barnyard was a scene of chaos with sheep, horses, <u>geese</u>, and goats all <u>running</u> loose.

B.   The carpenters were <u>using</u> thinner pieces of paneling because they were more pliable.

C.   Our new <u>neighbors</u> brought us some lettuce, <u>tomatoes</u>, and <u>dried</u> herbs from their organic garden.

D.   Because the college's <u>enrollment</u> keeps increasing, more dormitories must be built.

E.   Some very <u>weird</u> <u>occurrences</u> have been reported at that deserted beach.

32.1   WRITING OR SPELLING NUMBERS

Note: Corrected words/numbers are underlined.

A.   LaRue estimated that <u>15</u> percent of the class had failed the quiz.

B.   To get ready for the big race, Henry ran <u>three</u> miles one day, <u>five</u> miles the second day, and <u>eight</u> miles the next.

C.   We purchased <u>10</u> three-pound packages of chicken for the barbecue.

D.   The average grade on the calculus test was <u>62</u> before the professor applied the curve.

E.   We couldn't believe that it cost <u>forty</u> dollars to attend the <u>two</u>-hour concert.

32.2   USING ABBREVIATIONS AND ACRONYMS

Note: Corrected words/abbreviations/acronyms are underlined.

A.   We saw many amazing animals—elephant seals, otters, sea lions, pelicans, <u>and others</u>—on our trip to Monterey Bay.

B.   The <u>FBI</u>, the <u>CIA</u>, and <u>FEMA</u> aren't held in the highest regard by the American public.

C.   Uncle Steve moved from Reno, <u>Nevada</u>, to Huntsville, <u>Alabama</u>, last year.

D.   Martha Stewart has a good recipe for dumplings on <u>page</u> 9 of her latest cookbook.

E.   We measured the plot in meters, not in <u>yards</u>.

32.3   REVIEW EXERCISE: NUMBERS, ABBREVIATIONS, CAPITALS, AND APOSTROPHES

Note: Corrections and changes are underlined.

A.   One of the greatest dangers facing space travelers today is a swarm of human-made particles orbiting the earth. <u>On one of its missions, 106</u> particles struck the space shuttle *Columbia*. In an effort to avoid these dangerous projectiles, the U.S. <u>Space Command</u>, located in Colorado Springs, <u>Colorado</u>, tracks every piece of space junk that is any larger than <u>2.5</u> inches in diameter. At present, there are about <u>nine thousand</u> pieces of debris this size in orbit around the earth. Some of them are moving dangerously fast, up to 17,000 <u>miles per hour</u>. At this speed, a projectile that weighs one <u>ounce</u> can create an <u>eighteen-inch</u> hole in a sheet of steel that is <u>one</u> inch thick. <u>Researchers</u> continue to work on creating better armor plating for spacecraft, but avoiding contact with deadly particles is the best way to avoid disaster.

Adapted from James R. Chiles, "Casting a High-Tech Net for Space Junk," *Smithsonian* 29.10 (1999): 46–55.

34.1   COUNT AND NONCOUNT NOUNS

A.   The dog across the street was howling all night.

B.   Eric will study physics in graduate school next year.

C.   Correct

D.   Northern Washington State has lovely scenery.

E.   John is hoping to find employment in the service industry.

34.2   ARTICLES AND POSSESSIVE AND DEMONSTRATIVE ADJECTIVES

Note: Words that have been changed or added are underlined. Deletions are not shown.

A.   The line of tourists at the White House was already quite long, winding along the street next to the White House lawn called the Ellipse.

B.   I walked around the Ellipse and up a small hill to the Washington Monument.

C.   The line there was not as long, so I waited under the circle of fifty flags, one for every state in the United States.

D.   From the information in my guidebook, I learned that this monument is 555 feet tall and was the tallest structure in the world when it was built in 1886.

E.   After climbing to the observation area at the top of the monument, I could see all of the Washington area spread out before me.

34.3   SHOWING QUANTITIES OF NOUNS

A.   Mother bought plenty of groceries to feed the guests.

B.   However, she forgot the bag of flour at the checkout counter.

C.   The butcher told her that several kinds of beef were good.

D.   He also recommended buying some fish fillets.

E.   Now we have many choices of foods for dinner.

34.4   PROGRESSIVE VERBS AND VERB COMPLEMENTS

A.   The plane was taking off as the rain began to fall.

B.   I was sick all last week.

C.   John knows how to return to the campsite.

D.   She was still looking for her glasses when the movie started.

E.   They are eating lunch in the kitchen now.

34.5   VERBS FOLLOWED BY GERUNDS AND INFINITIVES

A.   Don't delay sending your money for the tickets.

B.   I now remember leaving my sweater at your house last night.

C.   We wanted to learn more about the Spanish Inquisition in history class.

D.   I will not deny running the red light, but I hope that the police officer didn't notice me.

E.   Luis persuaded his mother to allow him to borrow the family car for the weekend.

34.6   MODAL VERBS

Note: The correct verb form to be inserted in the blank of each sentence is underlined.

Possible answers:

A.   If I had written to you sooner, you would have known about the delay in our travel plans.

B.   I must wash the floor before my guests arrive.

C.   When we went to the beach every summer, we would build huge sand castles every day.

D.   We must finish fertilizing the lawn before it rains.

E.   Myrtle said she might go to Florida this winter.

34.7   TWO-WORD VERBS

Note: Words to be inserted in the blank for each sentence are underlined.

A.   John's old car often breaks down on long trips.

B.   Michelle picked out the nectarines without bruises at the farm stand.

C.   Don't put off until tomorrow what you can do today.

D.   I could not figure out how to solve the math problem.

E.   You must hang up the phone before you can receive a fax.

34.8   FORMING CORRECT VERB TENSES

Note: Correct verb forms are in bold.

A.   Before I registered for an 8 a.m. class, I **used** to sleep until noon.

B.   Rosalie nervously **smoothed** the wrinkles of her dress before returning for her encore.

C.   Our office **changed** to a new computer system last month, but most of the employees haven't figured out how to operate it yet.

D.   I felt **obliged** to attend Raoul's poetry reading although I really don't like his poetry.

E.   Books began falling to the floor when I **moved** the bookshelf away from the wall.

34.9   PLACEMENT OF ADJECTIVES

A.   We are finally planning to replace the old avocado-colored porcelain sink in our rustic kitchen.

B.   Father Poulos plans the giant annual Greek Orthodox Easter picnic in the largest town park.

C.   When we went to the car dealership, we saw many expensive red cars, but we wanted an inexpensive white car.

D.   That was the most depressing Danish movie that I've ever seen!

E.   Correct

34.10   PARTICIPLES AND NOUNS AS ADJECTIVES

Note: Correct verb forms are in bold.

A.   The **thrilling** end of the ballgame made us all go home feeling **exhilarated**.

B.   I am always **annoyed** when she tells those **boring** stories about her childhood.

C.   Denise must pay a well-**deserved** fine for returning the **library** books so late.

D.   One of my most **embarrassing** moments was accidentally setting off the alarm one morning before the store was open.

E.   Ramon reluctantly brought home his **disappointing** first-semester report card to his **waiting** parents.

34.11   PLACEMENT OF ADVERBS

A.   My family moved around the block last year.

B.   Thomas never asks for help with his writing.

C.   That is the most depressing news I've heard in a long time.

D.   Claire waited near the fountain a long time for Kurt.

E.   Correct

34.12   PREPOSITIONS AND PHRASAL PREPOSITIONS

Note: Words to be inserted in the blank in each sentence are underlined.

A.   Bob ordered fajitas <u>instead of</u> tacos.

B.   When the temperature falls <u>below</u> zero, I think <u>about</u> moving to a warmer climate.

C.   Meet me <u>at</u> 3 p.m. <u>at</u> the grocery store.

D.   I read <u>about</u> the Senate hearings <u>in</u> *Newsweek*.

E.   We took the mountain road <u>in spite of</u> the severe weather warning.

35.1   SENTENCE PATTERNS

S   AV   IO   DO

A.   The court sent the witness a subpoena.

LV   S

B.   Here are some letters for you.

S LV PA

C.   Sharon was short for someone her age.   (Correct)

S   AV   IO   DO

D.   The waitress brought the hungry customers some soup.

S   AV   DO

E.   The meteorology students visited Mt. Washington yesterday.

35.2   DOUBLE NEGATIVES AND DOUBLE SUBJECTS

A.   The new video games are very expensive.

B.   There are never empty seats on the bus at rush hour.

C.   I forgot that your cousin doesn't know my address.

D.   The dermatologist gave my mother some lotion for her rash.

E.   We seldom get much mail.

35.3   OMITTED WORDS

A.   *War and Peace* is a very long novel; it tells about Russia in the nineteenth century.

B.   As you know, there are many Internet providers for e-mail.

C.   Pit bulls sometimes are [*or* can be] very dangerous animals.

D.   It is healthy to get fresh air daily.

E.   Some rare paintings have been stolen from museums; they can never be replaced.

35.4   CONDITIONAL SENTENCES

Suggested revisions:

A.   When the lake freezes over, ice fishermen <u>set</u> up their ice houses and wait for the fish to bite.

B.   Unless you have a lot of money, you <u>should</u> not <u>move</u> to this area.

C.   Whenever it rains, the roof <u>leaks</u> badly.

D.   When we heard the whistle, we <u>started</u> running toward the finish line.

E.   If you purchase this warranty, your money <u>will be refunded</u> if the product is defective.

35.5 DIRECT AND INDIRECT QUOTATIONS AND QUESTIONS

A.   My cousin Betty asked if I remembered the summer we spent on Martha's Vineyard.

B.   The teacher warned the students not to come unprepared for the exam.

or

The teacher warned the students to come prepared for the exam.

C.   Bruce asked where the whales went in the winter.

D.   When we arrived two hours late, Uncle Samuel asked why we had sat in traffic instead of taking the back roads home.

E.   The police officer angrily asked the children defacing the traffic signs if that activity was their idea of a good time.

36.1 USING IDIOMS—SET 1

Note: Idioms are underlined and suggested translations are in boldface.

A.   Derek announced that he had read a 600-page novel last night, but I took this information with a grain of salt. (**was skeptical about the truth of this information**)

B.   The camp counselor told jokes to break the ice at the orientation meeting. (**make people feel comfortable/start a conversation**)

C.   Jeannie was floating on air after Marco asked her for a date. (**feeling very happy**)

D.   Olivia gave me the cold shoulder because I hadn't voted for her for class president. (**ignored me**)

E.   Mrs. Morin gave me the benefit of the doubt when I said that I couldn't finish my essay last night because my printer had run out of ink. (**chose to believe me even though my excuse sounded like it might not be true**)

36.2 USING IDIOMS—SET 2

Note: Idioms are underlined and suggested translations are in boldface.

A.   Dad warned us not to go overboard when buying refreshments for the party. (**not to be too extravagant/spend too much money**)

B.   My adviser said I should put my best foot forward at the job interview. (**do the best I can do**)

C.   Alonzo kept beating around the bush before finally admitting that he had lost my car keys at the beach. (**avoiding discussing the issue**)

D.   Don't rock the boat when the issue comes up for a vote. (**cause trouble**)

E.   I had a rude awakening when I opened my paycheck. (**an unpleasant surprise**)